FUEL YOUR FIRE

200 WAYS TO INSTANTLY BEAT BURNOUT AND REIGNITE YOUR PASSION

SAMANTHA ACTON

Adams Media
New York   London   Toronto   Sydney   New Delhi

Aadamsmedia

Adams Media
An Imprint of Simon & Schuster, Inc.
57 Littlefield Street
Avon, Massachusetts 02322

First Adams Media trade paperback edition January 2020

ADAMS MEDIA and colophon are trademarks of Simon & Schuster.

For information about special discounts for bulk purchases, please contact Simon & Schuster Special Sales at 1-866-506-1949 or business@simonandschuster.com.

The Simon & Schuster Speakers Bureau can bring authors to your live event. For more information or to book an event contact the Simon & Schuster Speakers Bureau at 1-866-248-3049 or visit our website at www.simonspeakers.com.

Interior design by Julia Jacintho
Interior images © Simon & Schuster, Inc.

Manufactured in the United States of America

10 9 8 7 6 5 4 3 2 1

Library of Congress Cataloging-in-Publication Data
Names: Acton, Samantha, author.
Title: Fuel your fire / Samantha Acton.
Description: Avon, Massachusetts: Adams Media, 2020.
Includes index.
Identifiers: LCCN 2019038281 I ISBN 9781507212608 (pb) I ISBN 9781507212615 (ebook)
Subjects: LCSH: Burn out (Psychology) I Stress (Psychology)
Classification: LCC BF575.S75 A285 2020 I DDC 155.9/042--dc23
LC record available at https://lccn.loc.gov/2019038281

ISBN 978-1-5072-1260-8
ISBN 978-1-5072-1261-5 (ebook)

Contains material adapted from the following titles published by Adams Media, an Imprint of Simon & Schuster, Inc.:
5-Minute Bliss by Courtney E. Ackerman, copyright © 2019,
ISBN 978-1-5072-1047-5.
5-Minute Energy by Isadora Baum, copyright © 2018,
ISBN 978-1-5072-0882-3.
1001 Ways to Do Good by Meera Lester, copyright © 2008,
ISBN 978-1-59869-474-1.
My Pocket Positivity by Courtney E. Ackerman, copyright © 2018,
ISBN 978-1-5072-0850-2.
My Pocket Yoga by Adams Media, copyright © 2017,
ISBN 978-1-4405-9944-6.

CONTENTS

INTRODUCTION

Do you feel overwhelmed and exhausted?
Are you finding it difficult to accomplish daily tasks?
Are you so stressed that you're not sure
you can make it through the day?

If so, you may be experiencing burnout. Burnout—that overwhelming feeling of exhaustion, frustration, and stress—is becoming more and more commonplace in today's world, but that doesn't mean you have to live with it. With *Fuel Your Fire*, you'll find two hundred exercises that can help you battle burnout and come away feeling refreshed, renewed, and relaxed.

The exercises in this book are targeted to fighting the mental, emotional, and physical exhaustion of burnout—because burnout doesn't just affect one area of your life, its influence infiltrates all aspects of your day. Inside, you'll find exercises aimed at calming your mind, disconnecting yourself from stress, relaxing your body, connecting and sharing joy with others, and finding peace.

These quick and easy activities will help you to both recover from the symptoms of burnout that may already be affecting your daily life and prevent future burnout from occurring.

Taking care of yourself both mentally and physically is your best defense against burnout, and with the activities and exercises in this book, you can do just that. *Fuel Your Fire* will help you find your joy, confidence, and purpose so that you can live a healthier and happier life.

Chapter 1

GETTING FROM BURNOUT TO
⇒REIGNITED⇐

What Is Burnout?

Burnout is a condition that affects tons of hardworking and high-achieving people—in fact, it is *especially* common in hardworking, high-achieving people. You'll know you're experiencing burnout when you feel the three hallmarks: feeling physically and emotionally exhausted, being distracted and inefficient in completing your work or other daily tasks, and feeling overly negative or disconnected from the people around you. There are other secondary symptoms (like dark rings or bags under your eyes, losing more hair than usual, and feeling irritable and short-fused with those you love), but these are the three big red flags for burnout.

If you have ever experienced this, you know that it just plain doesn't feel good to be burned out. Burnout is especially frustrating for people who are used to going above and beyond and smashing their productivity goals. When you go from getting things done early and sailing through your tasks for the day, to missing deadlines and feeling unable to focus, it can be confusing and upsetting, which only adds to the frustration.

Further, burnout can leave formerly passionate and engaged people feeling detached and apathetic about their work. It's almost as if burnout fills your emotional cup, leaving no room for other feelings. This is why so many people get burned out and mistake these symptoms for hating their jobs or no longer loving their work; when you burn out, it's not a sign that you don't care about or actively dislike your work—in fact, if anything it means that you may have cared about it *too much*!

How Does It Happen?

Burnout happens when we get so caught up in our work (or other meaningful projects) that we fail to manage the things that stress us out and forget to make time for ourselves. You might be handling all of your work and getting things done on time, but it's not healthy if you need to pull several all-nighters, cancel plans with friends and family, and neglect your self-care to make it possible. I'm sure you believe deep down that life isn't all about meeting deadlines—it's also about following your passion, having happy and healthy relationships with those you love, and growing as a person—but it can be surprisingly hard to live by that belief.

With today's technology, it's easier than ever to be constantly connected and always available. This makes for great customer service and lightning-fast response times, but it doesn't contribute to our mental health. Essentially, our increasingly digital world makes it so that we are always "on." At any time during the day, we are just one notification or phone call away from our work. This means that we never get any real breaks—you might take a day off, but if your cell phone is just a foot away and an email about work comes in, you can easily get sucked right back in to work mode.

However, even if you're successful in setting aside some nonwork time, you can still experience burnout. There are multiple factors that can contribute to burnout, including a hostile work environment, unrealistic expectations from your superiors, lacking any sense of control over your work, working with unfriendly or apathetic coworkers, or simply having more work than you can reasonably manage. Anything that makes your work unpleasant or overly difficult could be a contributing factor to burnout.

And don't make the mistake of thinking that if you don't have a high-stress, full-time job that you're safe from burnout! Stress comes from all areas of life, including work, hobbies, social relationships, family, and friends, among other things. It's well known that the burdens of caregiving can lead to burnout, putting at risk those who take care of children, older adults, or people with special needs. You can be a stay-at-home mom and be just as susceptible to burnout as a high-powered executive. We are all at risk of experiencing burnout if we don't make sure to take good care of ourselves.

What Can You Do to Prevent It?

So how do you take good care of yourself? What can you do to prevent burnout?

If you're thinking "self-care," you're absolutely right! Burnout and self-care are inexorably linked; burnout happens when you neglect your self-care, and self-care is what you need to combat burnout. However, when you're feeling under the gun and pressured to succeed, self-care is often one of the first aspects of your life to be cut short or skipped entirely, exacerbating the problem. Taking care of yourself gives you a chance to recharge, refocus, and enter a healthier state of mind.

However, self-care is not the only thing that can help. There are five vital actions you can take to prevent burnout.

Work On Your Self-Awareness

The first component of good defense against burnout is self-awareness. It takes a good amount of self-awareness to understand just how much is *too much* for you. You may find it easy to compare yourself to others, saying things like, "If he can put in 80 hours a week, so can I!" or "She works way harder than me and she's doing fine." That may be true—other people may be able to stay extraordinarily busy and also stay healthy—but that doesn't mean it's true for you. You might have an entirely different set of skills than the people you reference, along with different pressures, stresses, and systems of support. Comparing ourselves to others is generally an ineffective method of motivating ourselves. What is much more effective is meeting ourselves where we are at, and we need self-awareness to find out where we are.

Set Healthy Boundaries

It's extremely important to set good boundaries, and that goes for everything in your life. You should have clear and consistent rules about how you approach your work, your relationships, and anything else that takes up your time. Without boundaries, it's too easy to catch yourself thinking, "I can do a little more" or "I'll just answer one more email." Not only do you need to have healthy boundaries, but you also need to actually enforce them. If you have rules in place but frequently break them or make exceptions, you're not doing yourself any favors.

To ensure that you are protecting yourself from burnout, come up with some boundaries surrounding your work. These boundaries are up to you, but you might want to make rules like, "No laptop in bed" or "On my days off, I don't check my work email." These rules will keep you sane and happy, even if you're still in a high-pressure job or very busy during your working days.

Make Time for Sleep

You know that sleep is important, but it's often one of the first things to suffer when you get overwhelmed and over-worked. Getting a good night's sleep is not only going to help you avoid feeling sleepy and disengaged all day, it will also give you a boost in other ways. When you are well rested, you are better able to focus, more likely to be in a positive mood, and simply more productive.

You may not need the recommended 8 hours of sleep each night, but most people require at least 7 hours for optimal functioning. Invest in some blackout curtains, create a self-imposed bedtime, and put your phone on Do Not Disturb mode to set yourself up for success.

Don't Neglect Your Physical Health

Your physical health and your emotional health are closely linked; when you are physically unhealthy, you are much more likely to suffer mentally as well, and when your emotional health is threatened, you are susceptible to unhealthy behaviors. When you're feeling stressed, you may find yourself reaching for the ice cream or chips or hitting snooze in the morning instead of getting up and going to the gym. These urges are understandable—you try to find ways to cope with your stress, and junk food and sleeping in are two tantalizing options—but these coping methods are the last ones you should be using.

A healthy body makes for a healthy mind. You don't need to be a certain size or weight to be healthy, but you should aim to at least have a mostly healthy diet and get at least 30 minutes of exercise three times a week. If you don't have a gym membership, try simply going for long walks or taking a bike ride. In addition, don't forget to see your doctor regularly and pay attention to your body—it will tell you when something is wrong.

Build a Strong Support System

One of the best resources you have in dealing with stress and staying sane is a good support system. Everyone needs a shoulder to cry on or a word of advice now and then, and your support system is where you go to get it. Put some effort into your relationships with your family and friends to ensure they are healthy and happy. If you don't have many people in your support system, consider branching out, meeting new people, and making new friends. You don't need a ton of friends to reap the benefits, but you need to have at least a few strong relationships you can fall back on in tough times.

Having a strong network of meaningful relationships comes with an added benefit—the people who love you will be able to see when you start slipping with your self-care or taking too much on, and they will likely have something to say about it! Let people into your life, and they will help you keep yourself in check. Feed your relationships to feed your own mental health!

What Can You Do to Recover from Burnout?

If you're already feeling burned out, you have a tougher job: to recover rather than prevent. As with most diseases or illnesses, it's much easier to prevent them than it is to treat or cure them. But not to worry, that's where this book comes in!

In the rest of this book, you will find tons of suggestions, tips, and tricks on how to recover from burnout. They are organized into four main areas covering the major life domains:

- Refuel Your Body
- Refuel Your Mind
- Refuel Your Emotions
- Refuel Your Relationships

Refuel Your Body is all about moving, eating, and sleeping; in other words, this chapter will teach you healthy ways to treat and eradicate the symptoms of burnout in your body. Refuel Your Mind is focused on ways to manage stress, change your perspective, and reframe the way you approach stressors in life. Refuel Your Emotions will show you exercises to acknowledge your emotions, accept them, manage them, and feel positive emotions more often than negative ones. Refuel Your Relationships will give you concrete ideas to connect with others and build happier, healthier relationships with those around you.

It's important to remember that burnout is an all-encompassing condition, and it requires a holistic approach to recover from it—meaning you can't neglect any area of your life and expect to be able to combat the symptoms of burnout. One of these chapters may be more relevant than the others to you right now, but make sure you take some time to at least skim each of them, because burnout rarely leaves one domain untouched! For example, you might think that you're in pretty good health, but a visit to the doctor could reveal you may have a sneaky cholesterol problem. Or, you may think your relationship with your spouse is pretty solid, but after having a heart-to-heart, you may learn that your spouse has been suffering from the effects of your burnout. Remember to take care of your body, your mind, your emotions, and your relationships to give yourself the best defense against burnout.

Chapter 2

REFUEL YOUR =BODY=

Burnout can take its toll on your body. When your body is constantly bombarded with the stress signals caused by burnout, things tend to go haywire. The mental and emotional symptoms of burnout—when allowed to continue—become harmful to your physical body in ways such as loss of sleep, gastrointestinal issues, chronic fatigue, tight muscles in the legs and back, hunched shoulders, loss of appetite, frequent illnesses, and even teeth grinding.

Fortunately, the exercises in this chapter will show you fifty ways you can beat burnout in your body and feel rejuvenated and renewed. You'll find activities for breathing, moving, and even eating that will help you cope with the symptoms of burnout and safeguard your body against future burnout episodes.

TENSE TO RELAX

If you are feeling overly stressed out, it can be difficult to relax. You could spend hours trying to force yourself to relax to no avail. If you're finding it difficult to force yourself to relax, this exercise may help you find an alternate route to a feeling of tranquility in your body.

Find a quiet, comfortable, and private space. Dim the lights and turn off anything that might disrupt you. If you need some white noise to relax, try turning on a sound machine at a low level.

Lie on your bed or on a carpeted floor, and let your arms and legs rest wherever is comfortable. Close your eyes and begin breathing slowly and regularly. Follow these steps:

1. Direct your attention to your toes. Notice how they feel and whether there is any tension in them.

2. Squeeze and flex your toes as hard as you can (without hurting yourself), and hold the squeeze for 3 seconds.

3. Release your toes and allow all the tension to run out of them.

Once you finish relaxing your toes, move on to your feet, then your ankles, and so on until you reach your head. If you find that holding the squeeze for 3 seconds didn't release all the tension in one particular area, try holding for another 3 seconds in that same place.

TAKE A WALK

As simple as it sounds, taking a walk can battle burnout in big ways. It's a simple and easy activity that almost anyone can do when they want to feel better.

The next time you are feeling burned out, put on your walking shoes and go outside. If you're low on energy, try a quick, vigorous walk to put some pep into your day. A quick-stepping stroll will invigorate and energize you, leaving you with newfound motivation to carry on with your day.

If you're feeling overwhelmed or you've been multitasking all day, try a slow, purposeful walk. Force yourself to take a few medium steps instead of several small steps or one giant stride.

While you walk, remind yourself to look around you and enjoy the scenery. Notice any particularly appealing sights, for example, a tree with leaves waving gently in the breeze or a happy couple walking arm-in-arm down the street.

Whichever kind of walk you decide to take, keep some of your focus on your breath. Take in deep breaths through your nose, hold them for a moment or two, and let them out steadily through your mouth (for the energetic walk) or your nose (for the mindful walk).

Remember to give yourself a metaphorical pat on the back for engaging in a healthy physical activity, and thank yourself for doing something good for your mind and body.

ROLL AWAY THE STRESS

It's a well-known fact that we store stress and tension in our muscles, but you can ease this stress away with a foam roller. Grab a foam roller in preparation for this exercise. Pro-tip: If you don't have a foam roller lying around the house, you can substitute a pool noodle for some of the moves!

Think about where you hold tension in your body. Is it in your back? Or maybe your shoulders? Some people hold their stress where they sit, in their buttocks and hips. Wherever you find your stress, focus the foam roller there. For the purposes of explaining this exercise, we'll use the back as an example.

Start out by gently lying on the foam roller, but use your arms and legs to hold your body up and reduce the pressure on your muscles. Roll back and forth slowly, noticing where it feels best to release tension. Gradually introduce more pressure onto your muscles until it feels just a tiny bit uncomfortable.

As you feel the tension leave your muscles, feel it leaving your mind as well. Embrace this feeling and allow the stress to melt away.

TREAT YOURSELF TO SOMETHING DELICIOUS

It's important to feed your body the fuel it needs, and the fuel it needs is healthy food. However, it's also important to *treat yourself* at least once in a while! When burnout has you feeling down and depressed, try having an occasional treat to boost your mood.

Instead of choosing a snack based on its caloric content, its carbohydrate count, or the grams of sugar it contains, choose a snack solely based on how it tastes. Pick something you really enjoy and rarely let yourself eat.

Some delicious suggestions include:

- A cupcake
- A candy bar
- An order of hot, salty French fries
- A piece of cake
- A scoop (or two) of ice cream
- A small bag of crispy, kettle-cooked chips

As you eat your snack, keep your mind focused on how you feel. Savor the taste of your snack, and savor the feeling of treating yourself to something delicious. Thank your body for your ability to taste and enjoy food.

Try to indulge in these kinds of treats only once every couple of weeks. This will not only help you stay healthier, but it will also keep the experience feeling rare and special.

DANCE YOUR WAY TO FEELING BETTER

The overwhelming sensation of burnout can make you feel like you're drowning in everyone else's needs and can easily make you lose track of *who you are* and *what you are* feeling. Try this easy exercise when you need to recharge and get more in tune with your authentic self.

Stand up and move to a space where you have a lot of room around you to move freely. Take a few moments to think about your current mood.

Ask yourself questions like:

• What's on my mind right now?
• How am I feeling?
• How would I like to feel?

Consider your answers to these questions, and come up with a dance move that expresses who you are and your emotions in this moment. There are no rules for this movement, only that it must be in line with how you're feeling.

You can jump, skip, sway, dip, sweep, wiggle, wave, or flail. You can raise your arms, lift your knees, shake a leg, bow forward, lean backward, or do all of these moves in a sequence. You can move slowly or quickly; in a regular or an erratic pattern; in smooth or short, brisk movements— whatever matches your authentic self, right here and right now.

Don't worry about how you look. It doesn't matter whether you look graceful, sexy, or skilled in this moment. All that matters is that you are expressing and honoring your current state and your authentic self. When you are in touch with your authentic self, it's hard not to get a boost to your well-being!

TOUCH THOSE TOES

A good stretch can do more than release tension in your muscles and improve your flexibility; it can also help you to focus better, feel rejuvenated, and rescue you from burnout. To experience these benefits yourself, try this stretch:

1. Stand straight with your feet hip-distance apart and your arms at your sides.

2. Inhale deeply through your nose. As you inhale, raise your arms up over your head with your palms up, until they meet at the top.

3. Release your breath through your nose while you bend forward at the waist. Bend as far as you can without your back bowing or rounding. If you need to bend your knees to get a good stretch, go ahead and bend them.

4. Separate your outstretched hands, grasp your big toes (or hug your thighs or your calves close if you can't reach your toes), and hold this stretch for 10 seconds.

5. Release the stretch and stand up straight again with your arms at your sides.

6. Repeat this stretch at least three times, or as many times as you feel like repeating it.

Thank yourself for the stretch, and commit to carrying the sense of rejuvenation you feel with you throughout your day.

INDULGE IN A LUXURIOUS BATH

There's nothing that can feel quite as lavish and pampering as taking a long, relaxing bath. Even a short bath can have a profound impact on your mood and fight the effects of burnout.

- First, set the water to a warm, comfortable temperature and fill the bathtub. Don't make it too hot—you want to feel warm and cozy, but not like you're boiling!
- Turn off your phone, and lock your bathroom door.
- Clear out any clutter from the bathroom, and put your supplies (shampoo, conditioner, bath salts, maybe even a cup of tea!) within easy reach.
- Light some candles, and put on some soft and soothing music.
- Sprinkle the bath with some moisturizing oil, natural extracts, or bath salts. Use products that enhance the experience of the bath by making your skin feel extra smooth and soft, releasing a pleasant fragrance, or both.
- Breathe slowly and completely, focusing on the calm and the gentle feel of the water.

As you sink into the bath, let your state of mind match your physical state—give in to the relaxation and of the moment and let your stress slip away.

MAKE A FUNNY FACE

One of the new trends in looking younger, facial yoga promises to remove a few years' worth of wrinkles from your face. However, it may have a second, unintended benefit—battling burnout!

Give these facial yoga moves a try, and let the good feelings flow:

- **The Manual Smile**—Begin by adopting a gentle smile with your lips closed. Purse your lips slightly, then place your pointer and middle fingers on the corners of your mouth and pull the corners up toward your cheekbones. Hold this exaggerated smile for 30 seconds.
- **The Surprise!**—You know the universal "surprised" face? This move draws on that typical wide-eyed look. Open your eyes as wide as you can. Aim to show as much of the white of your eyes as possible, and hold this look for 30 seconds.
- **The Funny Face**—If you've ever tried to make a child laugh, you'll likely recognize this expression. Begin this exercise by putting on your surprise expression from the previous facial yoga move. Draw in a big breath, then blow all the air into your cheeks. Keeping your eyes wide and your mouth closed, alternate puffing air out from each cheek three times.
- **The Stick Out Your Tongue**—As the name implies, this expression involves only one thing: sticking your tongue out as far as it can go. Hold this pose for 60 seconds.

REACH FOR THE SKY

All stretches have the benefits of improving flexibility and releasing tension, but stretching upward can also help you feel open-minded, openhearted, and free from the stresses of burnout.

If you can, go outside for this quick stretch and follow these steps:

1. Stand straight with your feet hip-distance apart and your arms at your sides.

2. Inhale through your nose while you raise your arms above your head with your palms up. Let your palms meet above your head, and try to keep your arms straight.

3. Once your palms meet, turn them to the front and reach up as high as you can. You might get the urge to go up on the tips of your toes when you do this—feel free to indulge in that urge!

4. Hold the stretch for 10 seconds, breathing steadily in and out through your nose, then release the stretch and allow your arms to slowly fall back down to your sides, keeping your palms facing up until they reach your sides.

5. Take another deep breath in through your nose, and release the air out through your nose.

6. Repeat this stretch at least three times, or as many times as you feel like repeating it.

Remember to enjoy the stretch!

MOVE THAT BODY!

The link between physical activity and happiness is well established. Most people know that exercise releases endorphins (feel-good chemicals) in the body. Still, it can be difficult to get motivated.

For this exercise, don't think of exercising as a way to improve your physical health or your outward appearance. Instead, think only about the impact exercise has on decreasing your stress and making you feel happier. Don't worry if you can't commit to a 45-minute workout routine or to a 60-minute yoga class—just dedicate a few minutes to doing something active.

It could be a quick walk up and down the block. It could be 1 minute of jumping jacks. It could be doing a set of ten push-ups or holding Tree Pose for 1 minute on each leg.

It doesn't really matter what you do, as long as it involves movement. The point isn't necessarily to burn calories or to improve your heart health, but to get your brain working more positively and efficiently.

The next time you are struggling with burnout or just feeling plain down, try spending a minute or two doing something active. You might find that you enjoy the activity and want to continue doing it, or you might stop as soon as you can, but you will likely find that you got a little mood boost from your physical exertion.

GO OUTSIDE

Getting outside is good for you in so many ways. When you venture out, you get some fresh air, move your body, enjoy a change of scenery, and appreciate nature. Getting outdoors has another potential benefit you may not know: It helps you boost your resilience so that you can prevent burnout.

While you enjoy the sunshine and cool breeze, you are also opening yourself up to new ways of thinking. Just being outside can broaden your perspective and help you see past what's immediately in front of you. Strolling through nature encourages you to think outside the box and open your mind to all the possibilities the world has to offer. To take advantage of this nature boost, all you need to do is go outside!

Sometime during your busy day, make the time to spend at least a few minutes outside. Take a walk in the woods, jog on the beach, hike up to a waterfall, or simply stand outside and feel the sunshine on your face. When you come back inside, it might help to journal about your experience or to revisit the problem or issue you were thinking about before you ventured outside. You may find the problem is a little easier to solve than it was earlier!

If you find it difficult to get out every day, keep this suggestion in mind and put it to the test next time you are feeling burned out or stressed.

HAVE A DRINK

Is there anything as satisfying as a well-deserved, handcrafted drink at the end of a long, hard day? A favorite homemade cocktail or special tea can get you into a happier state of mind almost immediately.

To turn a simple drink into a burnout-battling exercise, just keep these three suggestions in mind:

- Instead of hurriedly making your favorite libation or ordering it from a waiter or bartender, make it yourself—mindfully. Stay focused on the task at hand and dedicate yourself to doing it well and with your full attention.
- Don't do anything else while you drink it. Just sit and experience your drink with no distractions. Leave the TV off and your phone in your pocket or purse; simply *be* for a few minutes.
- With each sip, remind yourself to savor the taste and the smell! Really taste the flavor, swirl it around in your mouth, and breathe in the aroma before you drink.

Remember, the drink doesn't need to be an alcoholic one! You can make any drink a rare or special treat.

TRY PRANAYAMA

Pranayama is the powerful, ancient practice of controlling your breath in order to direct the movement of life force (prana) energy through your body. It has been said that this type of breathing can help calm your mind and center your body. When the stress and fatigue of burnout has you feeling sluggish, try this exercise.

1. Sit or lie down in a comfortable position with your spine supported.

2. Close your eyes, or fix your gaze softly on a still object.

3. Inhale while expanding the belly area in three dimensions. Envision the breath going deep into the belly. As you do this, imagine the lower part of your entire torso expanding in three dimensions—to the side, the back, and the front.

4. Keep inhaling, and imagine the torso expanding at the level of the rib cage.

5. Continue to inhale, expanding the chest in front and behind to the shoulder blades.

6. Finally, as you exhale, allow the chest, rib cage, then belly to soften and relax your body.

CUDDLE WITH A PET

Pets don't know or care about stress, tension, or burnout—they just care about you! Spending time with your furry friend can have significant benefits, including making you feel happier, reducing symptoms of depression and anxiety, and even improving your physical health! Take advantage of these excellent benefits by spending a few minutes cuddling with your pet.

If you don't have a pet at home, think about someone in your life who does: Do your parents, siblings, or children have pets? How about a good friend or neighbor? Chances are, you know someone with a friendly pet who would be happy to loan him or her to you for a few hours.

In the time you commit to spending with your pet, focus on giving and receiving love. Most healthy, happy pets have a lot of love to give, and they're usually thrilled to get some back! Think about really making a connection with your pet through each touch. Look your pet in the eyes and enjoy the bonding.

Make sure you don't slip into absent-minded petting or mindless play; keep your focus on the warm, fuzzy connection between you and your pet, and you'll get a rush of good feelings to go with it!

RUN LIKE THE WIND

With all the stress and worry of adult life, it can be easy to forget what running can feel like to a kid: exciting, revitalizing, and exhilarating. Many of us haven't run in years or perhaps even decades. Others might run once in a while on a treadmill, but they may not find joy in performing this regular healthy-living task.

To recapture this feeling, challenge yourself to a quick run. It doesn't have to be far—and you don't have to time yourself—but you should try to run as fast as you can.

Remember the phrase "run like the wind"? Or perhaps you've heard the old descriptor that someone was "running like the devil himself was chasing them"? That's how you should run.

Throw your adult concerns about how you will look and what people will think to the side. Make the decision to run with abandon, revel in the feelings that running brings, and try to run so fast that all your cares and concerns are left in the dust.

Treat your inner child to "running like the wind"!

SAVOR YOUR MORNING COFFEE

Don't worry, if you don't drink coffee, you can also savor tea, juice, or any other drink or food you regularly consume in the morning! The coffee is not the important part of this exercise; starting your day with gratitude and peacefulness is what is important to set your day on the right track to avoid burnout.

Whether you usually make a beeline to the coffeepot as soon as you wake or you wait until you're heading out the door to pour your first cup, take a few extra minutes to sit and savor it before going on with your morning routine.

After you pour your cup and take a seat, direct your attention to all the pleasant things about your morning coffee. Before drinking, take a few moments to savor it with your other senses.

- Notice the warmth of the cup in your hand. Wrap both hands around it and enjoy the sensation.
- Notice the aroma wafting out of the mug. Lower your head, and breathe in the scent.
- Notice the sounds you are hearing, whether that's peaceful silence, chirping birds, or the sounds of your family getting ready for their day. Drink in the sounds and be grateful for what they represent.
- Notice the color of your coffee. Appreciate the deep, dark color of black coffee or the creamy, smooth color of a latte.
- Finally, take a sip. Close your eyes and savor the taste.

Taking a few moments to shift your busy morning routine and stop and appreciate your coffee will change the whole trajectory of your day and set you on the road to a positive day.

KISS SOMEONE

There's a reason why people all over the world engage in kissing—it's a natural and satisfying behavior that helps you feel closer to those you love and more invested in your relationships (and frequently acts as the precursor to some other intimate bonding behaviors!). It can also help battle burnout symptoms by improving your mood, signaling the joy receptors in your brain, and just making you feel more loved.

When choosing a loved one to smooch, make sure you pick someone you share a warm relationship with, someone who would be comfortable receiving a kiss, and someone whom you want to kiss. This person might be someone you kiss romantically—like your spouse or significant other—but it could also be someone you would give a more platonic smooch to, like a close friend or family member.

Pick your special someone and make sure to get their permission first, then smooch away! Bookend the kiss with a couple of hugs. While hugging your loved one, think about how much they mean to you and how much you appreciate the warm relationship you have with them. Thank them for the kiss and bask in the warm, fuzzy glow of happiness.

OPEN YOUR KI PASSAGES

When stress and tension are making your body tight, a quick way to relax your body and find calm is a breathing technique to open your ki passages. Ki is the life-force or living energy that connects to all that there is and sustains your life breath. (The Chinese refer to it as *chi*, while the Hindus call it *prana*.)

During hard times, it is critical for your health that you raise your vibration to make yourself more resilient, and one of the best ways to do this is to circulate more energy through your body. In order to have proper energy flow you must first make sure your passageways are open. The following exercise helps to open up your ki passages.

1. Sit upright with your spine straight.

2. Open your mouth, relax your jaw, stick out your tongue, and pant like a dog.

3. Continue this for several minutes. These in-and-out breaths will open up your belly and clear the ki passageways from the base of your spine to your throat's vocal cords.

GIVE YOURSELF A MASSAGE

It might not be as luxurious and relaxing as getting a massage from a professional, but getting a minimassage can have some wonderful relaxing benefits that also fight burnout, even if you're the one doing the work!

To get a little of that pampered feeling without the pampered price tag, sit up straight in a chair or on the edge of your bed. Take a deep breath in through your nose. As you exhale, place your hands on the tops of your shoulders with your palms down and your fingers pointing behind you.

Breathe deeply and regularly as you gently squeeze your shoulders. Move from the tops of your shoulders to the sides of your neck, then to the back of your neck, and even your shoulder blades—if you can reach them!

Next, cross your arms across your chest and give each of your arms a squeeze with the other hand. Rub your upper arms and lower arms in the same way.

Finally, finish your minimassage with a quick massage of each hand, focusing on the center of the palm. Take a deep breath through your nose and slowly and gently exhale through your nose to end the relaxing experience.

STRETCH LIKE A CAT

When burnout has your body feeling tense and rigid, stretching is one of the best things you can do to combat it. Try the Cat and Cow yoga poses. These poses are part of a breathing exercise, and they are intended to be alternated as you inhale and exhale. This combination of stretching and breathing is sure to relax your muscles and help you regain some calm.

To try these stretches, get down on all fours. A yoga mat or other soft padding might help your knees if the floor is hard. Start with a straight back and your head facing straight down toward the ground.

Begin with a deep inhale through your nose. As you inhale, arch your back like a cat and pull your belly button up toward your spine. Roll in as far as you can, until your head is facing your pelvis.

Hold this stretch for a moment, then exhale through your nose. As you exhale, move back down to a neutral spine, then roll into a curved spine. Drop your belly button toward the ground while keeping your hips and shoulders in roughly the same spots as before. At the same time, lift your head up to look at the sky.

Alternate between the Cat and Cow Poses for at least five breaths, and enjoy the sense of peace and calm the stretch brings!

STRIKE A POSE

When you feel stressed, you can start to lose confidence in your abilities. This loss of confidence can in turn cause your stress levels to increase and result in floundering to accomplish your daily tasks. To break this vicious cycle, try striking one of these simple confidence poses to make you feel like the confident rock star you are:

- Stand up straight with your legs hip-distance apart. Ball your hands into fists, and put them on your hips. Tilt your chin up, as if you were looking at something just over the horizon.
- Stand up straight with your legs hip-distance apart. Raise your arms in a V position, or as you would for the Y in "YMCA" dance.
- Sit at a desk or table with your legs hip-distance apart. Lean forward slightly, rest your elbows on the table, and fold your hands together in front of your chest with your knuckles facing up.

Keep this exercise in mind when you are starting to lose confidence, especially before a big presentation, job interview, or another nerve-racking situation.

FILL YOUR LUNGS

When you take a deep breath, you might think you fill your lungs all the way. However, the truth is there is usually a little bit of space left. This exercise will help you learn how to play with this space, use it to fight burnout, bring yourself more peace and calm, and revitalize your mental state.

Begin with a deep inhale through your nose. When you've reached the top of your inhale, pause for a moment, then take in just a bit more air. Pause again, and exhale all of your breath through your mouth. Pause for a moment when your lungs are empty and start again.

When you first try this exercise, use this routine: 5 seconds in, 1 second pause, top off, 1 second pause, 5 seconds out, 1 second pause. In other words, inhale deeply for 5 seconds, pause for 1 second, take in a bit more air, pause for 1 second, exhale for 5 seconds, then pause for 1 second once your lungs are empty.

Continue breathing this way for at least five repetitions. As you practice this exercise more often, challenge yourself to increase the pauses to 2 seconds each, then 3 seconds each.

HOLD HANDS

At the end of your workday or when you climb into bed at night, set aside a few minutes to just sit or lie next to your partner, connect physically, and tell each other about your day. You don't need to talk about any particularly weighty topics (unless you want to!). You can chat about interesting things you saw, heard, or did—just share what your day was like.

You also don't need to be pressed against each other from head to toe (again, unless you want to be, of course!). A small connection like holding hands can be effective in helping you feel in touch with one another.

In fact, the simple act of holding hands does a variety of burnout-busting things:

- It relieves stress.
- It boosts love and bonding.
- It lowers your blood pressure.
- It fights fear and relieves pain.
- It provides a sense of security and comfort.

The small physical and emotional connection you get from holding hands will give you an enduring sense of happiness in your relationship with your partner.

FIND CALM WITH THREE-PART BREATH

This exercise comes from the ancient Hindu system of medicine known as Ayurveda, which translates to "knowledge of life." This exercise is especially good for calming the mind and nervous system when burnout has you full of stress and tension.

1. Sit tall to lengthen your spine.

2. Seal your lips and relax your forehead, jaw, and belly.

3. Take steady, long breaths in and out through your nose.

4. Let your breath slow down so much that you can feel your belly, rib cage, then chest expand and contract with each inhalation and exhalation.

5. Take a few minutes to establish a relaxed and even breathing rhythm.

6. Next, begin to slow down and extend your exhalations, allowing them to become longer than your inhalations. To help lengthen your exhalations, gently contract your abdominal muscles as you breathe out.

7. Without straining, draw your navel back to the spine to create slow-motion exhalations.

8. Gradually build your exhalations to last twice as long as your inhalations. Stay relaxed as you gently contract your abdominal muscles to squeeze the air out of your lungs. Breathing this way helps to release strong emotions such as anger, frustration, and impatience.

9. Continue for 3 to 5 minutes.

CHALLENGE YOURSELF WITH A PHYSICAL TASK

Rest, relaxation, and comfort are all vital parts of your self-care. However, you weren't made for all rest and relaxation, either! It's extremely important that you stay physically active for both your physical health and mental health. One way to get a bit more active and fight the symptoms of burnout at the same time is to challenge yourself to some sort of physical task.

When you engage in a little competition, even if it's only competition with yourself, you often enjoy a burst of energy and motivation as well as a sense of satisfaction once you've finished.

To harness this revitalization, challenge yourself to a task that involves physical activity. It can be customized based on your health and activity level, and it could be anything from 5 minutes of sustained speed-walking to 5 minutes of pull-ups! The challenge itself doesn't need to meet any certain specifications, other than that it is truly challenging for you.

Are you up to your own challenge? Give it a shot!

SCREAM

Screaming can be incredibly liberating, and it can fight burnout by helping you to regain control in your life. First off, screaming is loud—the sheer volume will awaken your mind instantly. Second, when you scream, you feel empowered and strong, which can boost your energy levels and motivate you to seize control through the power of your voice.

Lift your arms in the air and spread them out to the sides until you resemble a starfish. Throw your head back and look upward. Take a deep breath and let loose! Let the relief overcome your entire body, and feel your mind start to wake up. Repeat for 5 minutes if needed, being sure to take a deep breath in between each scream.

You may want to check your surroundings before you begin—clearly screaming at the top of your lungs in your office cubicle or on a busy street might alarm people. If you're in a place where you can't let it all go, you can still scream lightly with your teeth clenched, so it still feels powerful, but much quieter. However, if you are in private and have some space to give the shout your all, go for it! Let out that pent-up tension to let go of worry and fatigue.

TRY ALTERNATE NOSTRIL BREATHING

This conscious breathing exercise is designed to get you feeling calm, collected, and free of stress and the symptoms of burnout.

Here's how to do it:

1. Gently fold in your index and middle fingers on your right hand toward your palm, leaving your thumb, ring finger, and pinky finger extended.

2. Use your right thumb to gently hold your right nostril closed and breathe in slowly through your left nostril.

3. Use your right ring finger to hold your left nostril closed and release your right nostril.

4. Exhale through your right nostril.

That's it! Now, repeat this breathing exercise six times. Make sure to keep your right hand in the correct position (as described in step one), and keep your breathing steady and regular. Don't speed it up or slow it down, and keep your inhales and exhales to a similar amount of time.

Practitioners of this method swear by its relaxing effects, so keep an open mind and give it a try!

GET CLEAN

Sometimes the best way to boost your mood is to get clean! Even if you're not particularly sweaty, dusty, or dirty, a shower or bath just hits the spot.

To take advantage of the mood benefits a quick bath or shower can provide to overcome burnout, simply set the temperature to your own customized sweet spot and hop in.

As you clean your external self, take a few moments to simply enjoy the feeling of getting clean. Think about how good it feels to clean yourself off after a long, sweaty, tiring day and extend this sense of cleansing to your mind. Allow it to wipe away the busyness and grime of your day.

When you step out and start to dry off, thank yourself for taking this opportunity to do some internal and external maintenance. Commit to pairing your internal and external maintenance more often and scrubbing your inside along with your outside. Show yourself some appreciation, and enjoy the feeling of being squeaky clean.

DO JUMPING JACKS

Getting your heart pumping can be a good way to beat the symptoms of burnout by enhancing positive feelings both in your body and about your body. To tap into those good feelings, set a timer for 1 minute and do some jumping jacks! Here's how:

1. Stand with your legs straight and your arms at your sides.

2. In one smooth motion (or not-so-smooth motion—that's okay too!), hop straight up and bring your feet out wide and your hands up above your head.

3. In another smooth motion, hop up again and bring your arms and legs back to their starting positions—legs together and straight and arms at your sides.

Continue doing jumping jacks for the full minute. It's okay if you don't get many in during that time; whether you do five or fifty jumping jacks, just make sure you give it solid effort.

When the timer goes off, stop the jumping jacks and spend a few moments noticing how your body feels. You are probably sweaty and out of breath, but you might also feel exhilarated, energized, and just a bit more confident. Enjoy those feelings and revel in the slightly-tired-but-invigorated sensation in your muscles.

TRY A NEW HAIRSTYLE

Sometimes it is the monotony of your day that can lead to burnout. Changing things up occasionally is healthy and fun and can bring you a renewed sense of joy. If you usually stick to the same hairstyle every day, this is a great opportunity to mix things up and try a new look.

If you usually straighten your hair, grab a curling iron. If you usually curl your hair, fire up a straightener. For those who always wear their hair down, get some hair elastics and bobby pins and prepare to put it up. If you're low-maintenance when it comes to your hair, pull out some products and/or any kind of tools you have lying around.

Stand in front of the mirror and play with your look for a few minutes. Try something elegant and timeless, something bold and fresh, or something completely crazy. You don't have to wear it that way all day, but it's fun to use a little creativity on a part of your life that can have such a strict and boring routine.

Take a look in the mirror and admire your new look. Be grateful for all your options when it comes to how you present yourself to the world!

SMILE!

Facial expressions are tied to how you feel. You flash a genuine smile when you're feeling good, and don a scowl when you're burned out. If your feelings can affect your facial expressions so easily, perhaps your facial expressions can influence your feelings!

To give it a shot, all you have to do is smile.

However, not just any smile will do; there are a few guidelines to help you do it right. You may be thinking, "Why would I need guidelines to smile?" Of course, no one needs to be taught to smile, but a forced smile is not the same as an authentic smile. Here's how you can produce an authentic smile:

- When you smile, allow the skin at the corners of your eyes to crinkle.
- Don't force your eyes to stay wide open—it's okay if they squint a bit.
- Show your teeth! Let your lips part and smile with your teeth showing.

If you have trouble with following these guidelines, there is a cheat: You can hold a pencil between your teeth! Holding the pencil in your mouth (horizontally) and gripping the pencil with your teeth pushes your mouth into the authentic smile position. When you just can't conjure up an authentic smile, give the pencil a try instead.

With either option, hold your smile for 1 minute and enjoy the boost to your confidence and mood!

RAISE YOUR ARMS TO GROUND YOURSELF

To beat burnout it is important to take a few moments each day to slow down and get in tune with your body. A good way to do this is to ground yourself. Here is an easy way to do that:

1. Stand with your feet directly under your hips. Plant your feet firmly on the floor, and stand tall to lengthen your legs and spine. Have your arms at your sides with your palms facing forward. Begin normal, relaxed breathing through the nostrils.

2. As you inhale, raise your arms slowly, feeling your belly fill up, then feeling your ribs expand and the top of your chest broaden with the breath. Let your expanding belly, chest, and ribs help you reach your arms up. At the top of the inhalation, the arms will be over your head with your palms out.

3. When exhalation naturally starts, lower your palms as you feel the breath leave the top of your chest and squeeze out of the lungs and the belly. Allow the lowering of your palms to help push the breath out of your body. Practice coordinating the lifting and lowering of the arms with the flow of the breath.

Do at least five breaths this way. Be aware of how you feel after this experience. Do you feel more grounded and internally connected? Are you calmer and more focused?

BEAT STRESS WITH GINGER

Studies have proven ginger's ability to ease cognitive stress, which can then free the mind and create more energy and focus. When there's less tension in the head, it's easier to fight fatigue during the day. Ginger also has anti-inflammatory powers, which fight disease and keep the heart healthy. In addition, it both boosts and maintains the immune system to prevent you from coming down with a case of the sniffles, and it can help mitigate symptoms of nausea and digestive discomfort. Basically, ginger is pretty darn handy to have on hand.

How can you get your stress-reducing ginger boost?

- Take a ginger supplement with a big glass of water.
- Rub a ginger-infused essential oil on your pulse points, such as the wrists, temples, neck, behind the knees, and ankles.
- Incorporate fresh ginger into your cooking (think stir-fry vegetables, ginger-glazed salmon, or a refreshing juice or smoothie).

No matter your method, take a few minutes to inhale the smell—it's very strong, so you're going to feel that jolt of energy instantly. Try a few meditative breaths, really savoring the aromas. You'll get an instant kick that will reawaken the mind, boost your mood, and make you feel more relaxed.

SING IT OUT

You don't need to be good at something to get joy from do-ing it. Singing is a prime example of this! Lots of us love to belt out our favorite tunes (whether in front of a crowd at karaoke or alone in the shower), but we're under no illusion that we'll be winning a singing competition any time soon.

For this exercise, you don't need to be good at singing—you just need to enjoy doing it!

To get an instant boost of joy to fight your burnout stress, blast your favorite song in the car or shower and sing along to it. Don't worry about what you sound like or how you look—just let yourself sink into the song and give it all your energy for a few minutes.

Singing can be so enjoyable, because you engage with your breath, with your body, and with your creativity, in addi-tion to connecting with positive memories and good feelings through your favorite songs. Take advantage of this unique experience by singing with all your heart!

MOISTURIZE YOUR SKIN

There's only one step between you and an instant mood boost for your fatigued body: some soft and silky moisturizer!

Most of us have at least a bottle or two of lotion lying around somewhere, and it's often just a quick hop over to the local drugstore or grocery store to pick some up if you're out. Grab some lotion and bare some skin, then follow these steps:

1. Start with a large area, like your legs or arms. Pour out a generous portion of lotion and start to gently and slowly work it into your skin.

2. As you spread the lotion over your skin, practice a bit of mindfulness. Pay attention to how it feels as your skin drinks it in. Notice the sensations as you gently rub the lotion in.

3. Continue applying lotion wherever your skin is dry, cracked, or in need of some softening.

4. As you finish up, imagine that your skin was parched and dying for some moisture, and that it is grateful for the relief you just gave it.

Revel in your silky smooth skin, and enjoy the sense of relaxation that comes with it!

GO FOR A BIKE RIDE

Getting outdoors, taking in some good views, and breathing in a little fresh air can do wonders for your mood as well as your body, which also prevents burnout from taking over. Taking a bike ride is one of the best ways to do this, especially if you're not a fitness enthusiast or if you're nervous about taking a long walk by yourself.

To give this exercise a try, simply hop on your bike and pedal off in a direction with something interesting ahead!

As you ride, focus on keeping your lungs open and your mind clear. Allow the beauty and peace of nature or the energizing rhythm of city life to fill your head and heart with happiness.

If you don't have a bike, you can substitute a stationary bike, whether you have one at home or you have to take a quick trip to the nearby gym. You won't get the nature and fresh air or revitalizing city ride aspects, but you can use it as an opportunity to practice visualization!

EAT SOMETHING DELICIOUS

Food lovers rejoice! This exercise is all about fully experiencing and savoring your food. When you take the time to slow down and appreciate something you are eating, you not only calm your mind and body, but you get a boost of happiness from the experience. Plus, you get to eat something yummy, which would make anyone happier!

First, grab something to eat. Ideally you should pick something you can eat with your hands, like an apple or a peach, but any food you love will do.

If you can, hold the food in your hands or lift it up on a utensil. Study the surface, noticing the shape and color. Look to see if it has a pattern or a grain to it.

If you are holding it, feel the food with your fingers. Notice the texture, whether it's hard or soft, rough or smooth. Notice the weight of it in your hands.

Next, move to smelling it. Hold it up to your nose and inhale deeply. Take a few breaths like this and experience the scent.

Now, take a bite. Notice the texture against your lips, the inside of your cheeks, and the roof of your mouth. Feel the texture with your tongue.

Notice the taste, whether it's sweet or sharp or tangy or salty. Be aware of whether the taste changes as you eat—perhaps it's tart at first, but the taste mellows out as you chew.

Continue eating mindfully until you have finished your food. Repeat this exercise as often as you'd like to boost your mood and calm your mind.

STRETCH YOUR NECK

The neck holds much tension, so relieving that stress can set you up for a more energetic and enjoyable day ahead. It's really easy to give your neck a good stretch, but be careful not to extend or hold positions for too long, since that can cause strain. You need to know your limits and move slowly, checking in to see if there's any pain. If so, stop. Here's a great activity to do:

1. Stand with your feet hip-distance apart and your arms at your sides. Reach both hands behind your back, using your right hand to hold on to your left wrist.

2. Using the pressure from your right hand, gently straighten your left arm behind you, away from your body.

3. At the same time, move your right ear toward your right shoulder, where you should feel a stretch in your neck.

4. Stay in this pose for 30 seconds. Repeat on the other side, using the left hand to pull the right arm away from your body, moving your left ear toward your left shoulder, and hold for 30 seconds again.

Do this exercise for a total of 5 minutes—you'll leave with a kink-free neck, less tension, and a little more energy!

DO PUSH-UPS

To really fight the stress of burnout and give a boost to your energy level, your mood, or anything else—try push-ups.

Find a spot on the floor that's clear and drop to your hands and knees. Next, follow these guidelines to ensure that you don't cheat yourself by doing halfhearted push-ups.

1. Try to keep your body as stiff and straight as possible; push your tailbone down (so your butt isn't sticking up) and keep your calves and thighs parallel to each other and to the ground (so your knees aren't bent).

2. Make sure your shoulders aren't drawn up toward your ears. Keep them in a natural position.

3. Keep your elbows in by your sides to ensure good posture.

4. Fix your gaze on something a couple feet ahead of you on the ground so that you're looking a bit ahead rather than straight down. This will help keep your neck in proper alignment.

5. Slowly allow yourself to move toward the ground, don't let your arms bow out or your butt float up toward the ceiling.

6. As you push yourself up again, try not to go too fast or in jerky motions. The ideal motion is a smooth one, with just a hint of a pause at the top.

Try to keep all of these in mind. Improper exercise is a waste of your time, because you won't be reaping the benefits of your effort. Don't waste your own time, and honor your effort by committing to proper form!

SIT UP STRAIGHT

How you hold your body can make quite a difference in your level of tension. If you want to fight burnout and fatigue, pay attention to your body and practice good posture. Here are some things to check on:

- Are you slumped over? It's hard on your back when you have an unnatural curve or hump in your spine! Focus on sitting up straight. If it helps, pretend you have a balloon tied to the top of your head, lifting your whole body straight up.
- Are your ribs out of alignment with your hips? If you're slouching or leaning to one side for too long, you can put unnecessary pressure on your back and muscles. Make sure your resting, default position is with your ribs directly over your hips.
- Are your shoulders hunched forward, sagging downward, or uneven? Set your shoulders above your hips, parallel and even, and keep your shoulder blades flat on your back. This will not only help you feel better physically, but it can also help you feel more confident and capable.
- Are your legs folded to one side, dangling toward the ground, or forcing your knees up above your hips when sitting? If so, you might want to switch up the settings on your seat or try to make a few changes to your seated posture—especially if it's your chair at work or at home or another chair you spend a lot of time in. Make sure your feet can rest flat on the floor in front of you and your knees are roughly level with your hips.

PLAY A GAME

Want a fun and easy way to let go of some adult worries? Try playing a game.

Think about how often you see children playing games. Children are naturally playful, curious, eager to learn new things, and at least a little competitive, which leads them to a built-in love of games.

Now think back to when you played games as a child. You probably really enjoyed your time playing games. In fact, some of your most favorite memories might involve playing a game, like Monopoly, tag, or hide-and-seek.

Decide to chase a little of that happy feeling again as an adult—and use a game to do it.

It might be best to play a game with your child or another child you spend time with often, but it's not a requirement.

Pick the game you found most enjoyable as a kid and dig it out of the closet or find a way to play it online. Let yourself sink into the game and let go of all your adult worries.

Allow the game to distract you from the stress and pressure of being an adult and remind you what it's like to feel effortlessly happy.

PUT YOUR TOES IN THE SAND

There's nothing quite like the beach: the sound of waves crashing, the smell of ocean in the air, the breeze that brings you some of that salty sea spray. Just picturing it can make you feel the stress slipping away!

Put the magic of the beach to work for you by finding a little bit of sand. If you're near a beach, that's clearly the best place to find some sand for this exercise. If not, see if you can find a bit of sand somewhere else—a sandbox at a playground, the sandpit at the local park, or even some vaguely sand-like dirt outside your house!

Follow these steps to get some beachy bliss:

- Take your shoes and socks off, if you're wearing any.
- Sit or stand with your feet in the sand. Direct your attention to the sensations in your feet; wiggle your toes and rock back and forth on the balls of your feet.
- Close your eyes and visualize the beach. See the sand and the water, smell the salty air, and hear the waves rolling in and out.

Stay here for a few minutes and soak in the happiness of a (virtual) beach day!

SQUEEZE A STRESS BALL

This may sound like an elementary way to battle the stress of burnout, but if you've ever squeezed a stress ball before, you know that it can be immensely satisfying! There's something about the squishy, rubbery feeling complemented by the slight resistance that strips away your stress, clears your mind, and helps you feel happier.

If you're not sure what the fuss is all about when it comes to stress balls, try these exercises and see for yourself:

- **Simply squeeze!** Tighten your hand around the ball until you feel real resistance.
- **Roll the ball in your hand.** This will help you improve your dexterity and facilitate problem-solving.
- **Toss the ball from one hand to the other.** Not only will you practice your fine motor skills, but you will also get a boost in brainstorming and idea generation.
- **Hold the ball between two fingers at a time, squeezing slightly.** This will give your fingers a rare workout and help you clear your mind.

Something as simple as a squishy rubber ball can have a surprising impact on your state of mind and help you to feel relaxed and rejuvenated.

GIVE YOURSELF A LOVING TOUCH

We often show others we love them through touch. We give our friends and family members hugs, kiss them on the cheek, hold hands with our significant other, and give a back rub or neck massage when we're feeling especially generous.

This physical gesture of love can be extended to yourself as well as to those you love. The next time you are feeling burned out, stressed, upset, or worried, soothe yourself with a loving touch.

Try any of the following touches, or go with whatever works best for you:

- Place one or both hands over your heart and rest them there for a few breaths.
- Give yourself a hug, placing your hands on your shoulders.
- Use one hand to gently hold the other.
- Stroke one arm with your opposite hand for a few minutes.
- Place a hand on each cheek and gently cradle your face.
- Wrap your arms around your belly and give a gentle squeeze.
- Run your hands through your hair or over your head in a gentle caress.
- Run your nails lightly down your neck and/or over your shoulders.

You may feel a little self-conscious at first, but these are all excellent ways to battle stress or worry by showing yourself a little bit of love.

SQUISH SOME PLAY DOUGH

Here's a way to beat your stress, find some surprising calm, and enhance your happiness by engaging your inner child: Play with play dough!

Do you remember how fun it was in elementary school when they broke out the play dough? In my classroom, it was like Christmas had come early!

To make your inner child smile, pick up some play dough from the store (If you're feeling super artistic or industrious, you can search for a recipe online and create your own). Take a minute to just play with it and enjoy the feeling of the play dough in your hands.

Playing with this squishy, moldable substance is a great way for children to boost their hand–eye coordination, improve dexterity, and prepare their hands for those fine motor skills they will soon be learning in school. Luckily, it also has some great benefits for adults—it can boost your creative thinking, keep fidgety hands busy, and help you clear your head and find some extra joy!

HYDRATE YOUR BODY

A simple but vital way to take good care of your body is to make sure you are hydrated. It also gives you an opportunity to enjoy the heavenly feeling of quenching your thirst with clear, cool water!

If you feel tired, drained, stressed out, or even a little moody, give hydration a try. It's a pretty simple two-step process:

1. Pour yourself a full glass of water and drink it!

2. Repeat until you are no longer thirsty or you feel like your belly will slosh around with every step.

It can be easy to forget to hydrate with everything else going on in your busy life, but the benefits justify putting in a little extra effort to keep hydration in mind.

After you've hydrated, take a moment to think about how you feel now. Do you feel a little less tired, drained, moody, or stressed? Don't be surprised if some of your bad mood or fatigue melted away! Keep that in mind next time you find yourself in need of some something to boost your mood.

TWIST

One of yoga's best contributions to reliving tension in the body is the twisting it incorporates. Twists are movements we don't naturally engage in very often, meaning that just a little twist can make a big difference in how we feel!

To get your mood-boosting, body-pleasing twists on, try these steps:

1. Lie flat on your back with your arms at your sides and your feet hip-distance apart.

2. Bring one knee up to your chest (or as close as you can comfortably get it to your chest) and, using your opposite hand, gently guide it to the other side of your body.

3. Keep your back flat and your shoulder blades pressed into the ground as you twist.

4. For an extra stretch, turn your head to the opposite side (e.g., if you bring your right leg up, use your left hand to guide it to the left side of your body and turn your head to the right).

5. Hold for at least 30 seconds or a full 2 minutes, then repeat on the other side.

STRETCH YOUR BACK

The back holds on to so much tension, and it is particularly affected during burnout. Unfortunately, since your back affects your body's alignment and your posture, back pain can throw your whole body off. The best way to prevent back pain is to stretch it in the afternoon when you're especially prone to cramping up. Here are some back stretches to try:

- Stand and place your hands, palms spread wide, on your lower back, right above your hips. Place them firmly with your fingernails pointing down toward the floor. Then lift your back and spine upward, pressing your shoulders down. You'll feel a great stretch in the back, opening up any tight muscles and getting in a full breath too.
- Stand and clasp your hands together behind your back. Lift your torso up, standing tall and proud. Push your arms and hands down toward the floor to feel that stretch. Then raise your clasped arms over your head, with your arms along the ears. Lift up with your torso and lean toward the right side, with straight arms clasped overhead and tilting to the right as well. Repeat this on the left side.
- Go on all fours and curl your back so it's moving upward, with your head loose and hanging below. Ease any tension in the neck by keeping it loose as well. Hold for a few seconds. Return to neutral, then arch your back so your head is straight and you're looking directly ahead. Alternate a few times. This exercise is very calming, so it will help center the mind and balance the body too.

These back exercises will create more blood flow in the body and alleviate stress.

TOUCH SOMETHING INTERESTING

Your mind and body are even more connected than you might think. Even small movements and actions can have a big impact on your thought process and your mood. So if you are feeling particularly stressed or burned out, try touching something new or unusual. It sounds small, but it can have a profound effect on calming your physical body.

Look around you and find an object that looks like it has an interesting texture or pleasant feel to it. You might pick a fun fabric, like velvet, satin, or something embroidered. You could also find an artistic décor piece that is slippery smooth; lumpy and bumpy; or has a rough, sandpapery surface. Take a peek and you're sure to find something that will feel interesting.

Take a few moments to simply feel the object. Pick it up (if it's small enough to pick up), or just sit beside it and explore it with your fingertips. Focus on the sensations you are experiencing, and simply enjoy the feeling of something new and interesting.

RUB YOUR TEMPLES

There's a reason massage therapists work on the temples during a massage. Rubbing the temples alleviates tension in the head, which can affect the entire body and change mood and energy states. The head holds a lot of weight, and when it's fatigued from burnout or the mind is burdened by negative thoughts, it drags you down. Applying pressure to the temples stimulates blood flow in the brain and relaxes the forehead, which builds energy and focus and banishes stress.

If you feel tired or stressed out, take a few moments to close your eyes and rub your temples gently. You can even combine the pressure with an essential oil to activate both touch and smell and further boost energy levels.

Some oils in particular have been proven to improve mental stimulation and awareness, such as peppermint, rosemary, basil, sage, lemon, jasmine, cinnamon, and juniper berry. Carry oils with you, or store them in convenient places in your office and home. Before using essential oils, speak to your primary care physician. There are certain rules regarding essential oil use for those with particular medications and conditions. For example, you might not be able to use them if you are pregnant or at too young of an age.

Chapter 3

REFUEL
YOUR
≥MIND≤

This chapter is about the metal exhaustion of burnout. Feelings of being overwhelmed by tasks at work or the responsibilities of family and home matters can leave you frustrated and fatigued. Often this burnout manifests itself as feelings of helplessness, being trapped, and an overwhelming sense of mental stress. The sense of self-doubt that this stress causes can lead to a pessimistic view of life and the world in general. When mental burnout has you feeling exhausted, taking time to manage your stress is paramount to overcoming it.

These exercises will help you shift your mental perspective from negative to positive. You'll find ways to challenge your current thinking and change your attitude from defeated to empowered. You'll learn about letting go of what is harming you, how to bring more positivity into your life, steps to take better care of yourself and your feelings, and ways to find calm and peace in your days.

ADJUST YOUR ATTITUDE ABOUT FAILURE

Pursuing perfection in all things is a quick route to burnout. If you're terrified to fail or ashamed whenever you don't reach your highest goals, it's time for an attitude adjustment! Failure is a fact of life. We all fail at some point, and you will fail too. This can be tough to accept, but think about the alternative: Can you imagine going through life with every single thing working out perfectly and in your favor? No one would want to read that book or see that movie, because it's boring! It's also completely unattainable and unrealistic to boot.

The next time you find yourself in a downward spiral about something that didn't work out right, read these statements about failure to yourself:

- Everybody fails, including me.
- Failure does not mean I am not good enough.
- Failure is not shameful or embarrassing; it means I was courageous and took a risk.
- If I never fail, I will never learn.
- "I failed" does not equal "I am a failure."

Read through these statements and allow them to sink in. Remind yourself of all the times some of the most successful people have failed (e.g., Steve Jobs, Walt Disney, Oprah Winfrey, Michael Jordan), and ask yourself whether failure is always such a bad thing. If you embrace failure as your teacher, it will not disappoint you. When you're free from the expectation of perfection, you're free to explore unknown ventures that can rekindle your passions and creativity.

TREAT YOURSELF WITH KINDNESS

Reframing your mind to think of yourself in a kinder way is an excellent first step toward beating the symptoms of burnout. We generally have little trouble uplifting, encouraging, and cheering up a friend, but we sometimes struggle to do this for ourselves.

Practice treating yourself like a beloved friend or family member to open yourself up to a happier and less stressful life. Here's how to treat yourself like a friend:

1. Imagine that a friend is sharing his or her troubles with you, and they happen to be exactly the same as your own.

2. Think about how you would respond to this friend. Would you tell him or her, "Too bad, so sad!" or would you offer a shoulder to lean on, words of encouragement, and assurances that he or she is loved and that he or she will make it through this?

3. Take the exact words, gestures, and compassion you would give to that friend and offer them to yourself.

4. Start to think of yourself as a friend. In truth, you are the one who knows you best, and you have the capacity to be the best friend you could ever have, so commit to acting like it!

THINK POSITIVELY

Studies have shown how positive thinking can work to improve energy levels, cognitive function, memory retention, and overall happiness. When your mind is weighed down with the negativity and anxiety of burnout, that stress can affect your body as well. When you are too caught up in negativity, you lose motivation, which can make you feel sluggish, insecure, and more prone to succumbing to defeat. However, spending just a few minutes a day engaging in intentional positive thinking can keep your brain sharp and troubles at bay, giving you a more energized outlook on life and its greatest pleasures. Here's an activity that will declutter your mind and free it from negative thoughts:

1. Think about what's troubling you. What thoughts and feelings are on your mind? What is causing you stress?

2. Close your eyes, and imagine these thoughts and words being swept away by the ocean. Let the waves take them away, somewhere far off in the distance.

3. Breathe in through your nose and out through your mouth. Take this moment to feel relief. Let out a sigh. Look forward to a fresh start. Open your eyes with new-found energy.

By taking a few moments to feel positivity abound, you'll feel invigorated, less stressed, and happier.

GIVE MINDFULNESS A TRY

Mindfulness is a wonderful tool. It can help you feel calmer, more focused, more relaxed, and just all around healthier. As it turns out, it can also make you feel less burned out and happier! If you've never engaged in mindfulness before, this exercise is a great way to ease into it.

1. Find a comfortable spot to sit or lie down. Settle in and close your eyes.

2. Allow your thoughts to come and go, your mind drifting from one to the next. Don't stop and focus on any of them, but don't avoid or ignore any of them either. As they pass, do your best to consider them without any value judgment (e.g., "I shouldn't feel this way" or "Wow, what a terrible thought to have!").

3. Spend a few minutes simply allowing your thoughts to pass in and out of your mind. If you find your mind wandering off on a tangent, simply direct it gently back to a nonjudgmental state.

4. If it helps, you can focus on your breathing. Feel each breath as it enters your lungs, fills your chest, and slowly escapes through your nose. Don't try to control it, just observe it and pay attention to how it feels to breathe.

5. When you're ready to end your practice, simply bring your awareness back to your surroundings and let go of any lingering thoughts. Allow your eyes to flutter open, and go on with your day as planned, but with one caveat—try to carry your relaxed and mindful state along with you.

REMIND YOURSELF OF THE GOOD

When you are feeling burned out, it can be easy to forget just how wonderful life is, but luckily it can be just as easy to remember the wonders of life—with a little nudge. When you stop and think about it, you'll see there really is so much to be grateful for, to be inspired by, and to revel in!

If the feeling of burnout is overwhelming you, and you feel inundated by bad news and negative events, stop and take a moment to remind yourself of the good. This includes things that make you feel joyful, blissful, inspired, proud, optimistic, hopeful, elevated, or *just plain happy*.

List your favorite things; think of inspiring stories you've read; and recall your own memories of kindness, bravery, and compassion. Remind yourself of the best things in life, and reflect on the incredible acts of goodness that people are capable of. Examples from your own life are most powerful in boosting your bliss, but don't worry if you can't come up with enough good things to focus on. There's lots of good news out there if you look for it!

If you find it exceptionally difficult to come up with a laundry list of good things from your own life or the lives of your friends and loved ones, check your local paper or scour the Internet for a recent news story about someone doing an extraordinarily good deed, read a poem by an inspirational author, or listen to a song that you find uplifting—whatever works to remind you of the good.

GIVE YOURSELF A BREAK

We often get so caught up in our day-to-day worries and tasks that we can forget to give ourselves a little time to breathe. Do yourself a favor and take a break from it all. Find a quiet spot to sit or go outside to enjoy the outdoors and simply take a few minutes to do nothing.

If it sounds like an easy exercise, that's because it is. However, that doesn't mean there aren't some helpful guidelines you can follow to make the experience a positive and effective one:

- Minimize any potential disruptions or distractions: This might mean turning your phone on silent, walking away from busy areas, or putting on some noise-canceling headphones. If you do decide to use headphones, avoid listening to music or anything else that could be distracting; the point is to mute the hustle and bustle around you and to discourage others who may be thinking about interrupting your break time.
- Turn off your inner critic: Don't let any voice saying, "You should really be working on Task A" or "Aren't you worried about Concern B?" break in. For the purposes of this exercise, you are your own boss, and the boss says it's break time. When you're on break, you don't have to think about any of that!
- Aside from the two previous guidelines, do whatever you want! Want to meditate? Great! Want to sit and daydream? Do it! Feel like staring into empty space? Go for it!

Taking a few minutes to do nothing can be surprisingly effective in making you calmer, cooler, and less burned out.

RELEASE YOUR "SHOULDS"

Have you heard of "shoulding"? It's a behavior that saps your happiness and opens you up to unnecessary stress and self-defeat. To make sure you are not heading down this stressful road that can quickly lead to burnout, try turning a "should" into a "can"!

First, identify some of your "shoulds." They are the implicit or explicit rules you have about how you should behave or how you ought to behave. We all have them, and they can be pretty sneaky.

Take a day to do this exercise prep if you need to: Carry around a journal and simply try to catch yourself shoulding throughout the day. When you do, write it down.

Now, the fun part—you get to turn those "shoulds" into "cans." For every "should," think about what would be more exciting, bolder, or more positive, and write the appropriate "can" statement underneath it.

For example, if your "should" is "I should always be agreeable, even when other people aren't," your "can" might be "I can respond to people with authenticity, even if it means I'm not the most agreeable person." Do this for every "should" and enjoy the blissful release of tension that comes with it!

PRACTICE POSITIVE AFFIRMATION

The negativity and doubt that come with burnout can strip energy from your mind, but fortunately, thinking positively can reverse the damage and shift your mentality.

A great way to encourage optimism is to do a positive affirmation activity. When you do this, you're basically using a cheery outlook to promote your self-worth and become more satisfied with your life. This in turn will provide a source of vitality in your life, and your brain will start to focus on what other wondrous things may be in store. Here is how to do it:

1. Think of something you love about yourself. Dig deep— is this something unique to you? How does it make you special? Why do you love this attribute in particular?

2. Think of an example of when you expressed this trait. Who did it influence? What was the outcome?

3. Think about how you can use this trait again in the future. Who would it affect?

This activity will help you feel energized and proud of the type of person you have grown to be. Give yourself credit for your achievements and positive traits on a regular basis, and you'll noticeably have less negativity and more happiness each day.

BUILD A BETTER RELATIONSHIP WITH MONEY

Money has a complicated relationship with burnout. The desire for it can lead you down a path of overwork and burnout, yet it is often seen as the goal for happiness. We all know that money cannot buy happiness. However, it's one thing to know it intellectually, and it's another thing to truly *believe* it.

To work on improving your relationship with money, go through this thought exercise:

1. Think about someone who would be described as rich but is not all that joyful. Ask yourself whether this contributes to the idea that money leads to happiness, or refutes it.

2. Consider someone you know or someone you've heard about who makes little to no money but is filled with joy and zest for life. Ask yourself whether this contributes to the idea that money leads to happiness or if it refutes it.

3. Imagine that you had all the money you needed to live a fairly good life; would all your current problems go away?

4. Imagine that a mysterious billionaire showed up to offer you $10 billion in exchange for making a huge sacrifice, like giving up your partner, never speaking to your family again, or losing your sense of taste. Would you accept?

If you're honest with yourself, you'll probably admit that there is little association between money and happiness. Remind yourself of this fact often, especially when you start to notice yourself obsessing about money.

SIT IN CHILD'S POSE

Balasana, also known as Child's Pose, is a yoga pose that can energize the mind and body, release tension, and provide greater balance. It can also give you more energy when you are feeling the fatigue of burnout. It's easy to do and has tremendous benefits for creating vitality throughout the body and boosting circulation. Here's how to do it:

1. Kneel on the floor, touching your big toes together. Then sit on your heels and expand your knees to about the width of your hips.

2. Breathe and lean forward, laying your body down between your thighs. Lengthen your tailbone by lifting your spine upward, and shift the base of your skull away from the neck. You should have full upper body expansion.

3. Extend your arms out in front of you so they are flat on the ground, and let your shoulders pull your shoulder blades across the width of your back. Breathe deeply in this pose.

4. Once finished, get out of Child's Pose by gently using your hands and walking your torso back to an upright position. Sit back on your heels.

You'll feel refreshed and centered, with more energy to tackle whatever's next on your plate!

LOOK AT YOURSELF WITH LOVE

If you're like a lot of people, you don't always like what you see in the mirror, and the depression and insecurities that accompany burnout can make this feeling even more pronounced.

We all have some insecurities and areas where we wish we could make some changes, but we should always be mindful of appreciating ourselves overall. That's what this exercise can help you do.

Go to the closest and most convenient mirror. Your bathroom mirror is probably a good choice, but any old mirror will do.

1. First, take a minute to simply look at yourself in the mirror. Don't make any particular expressions yet. Just take a good, long look at your face. Get to know it in a way that you haven't before.

2. Next, try saying a few positive affirmations to yourself. Make them healing thoughts that will help build your self-esteem and self-confidence. No negative talk allowed!

3. Now, give yourself a grin—a big, natural smile at yourself in the mirror. If you have trouble putting on a natural smile, think about one of your happiest memories and try to relive that feeling.

4. Note any laugh lines or smile wrinkles, the brightness in your eyes, the glow of your face, or anything else that acts as a visible reminder of your happiness and appreciate it for what it represents—a life filled with laughter!

TRY FULL-BODY RELAXATION

If burnout is causing you to have tension, stress, and aches throughout your body, there's nothing like a quick full-body relaxation practice to get you feeling happier, healthier, and more relaxed.

Start out by dimming the lights in the room you want to practice your relaxation in. Lie down on your back with your arms and legs resting wherever you find them most comfortable. If your lower back grumbles about lying flat, roll up some towels or grab a foam roller to place beneath your knees. This will take the pressure off your lower back and let you focus on truly relaxing.

Begin with a deep inhale through your nose. When you've reached the top of your inhale, pause for a moment and focus on one area of your body that is holding tension. Pause again, and exhale all your breath through your mouth while concentrating all your relaxation intentions on that area of your body. When your lungs are completely empty, pause for another short moment, then start over. Continue until you have sent relaxing sensations to every inch of your body.

When you run out of areas to focus on, continue breathing with this method and visualize big waves of calming, soothing energy washing over your entire body, beginning at the top of your head and gently flowing all the way down to your toes. Imagine this wave pushing out all of your aches and pains, all of your tension, and all of your worries.

SAY SOME STRONG WORDS

Pick a few words that evoke power and deeper meaning to you, then say them aloud with volume and authority. Let these words give you energy and strength when you're losing confidence. This practice is a great tool for both fighting and preventing burnout. Research has shown that thinking about power can in turn make you feel more formidable too. A few suggestions include:

- Strong
- Bold
- Leadership
- Bravery
- Poise
- Significance
- Resilience

Recite each word five times, but take a deep breath in between each utterance. This will allow your mind to register the word and your body to react. Go through five or so words total. After each word, think for a moment about how you feel—let yourself gradually radiate more self-assurance with each new recitation and word.

Ideally, you should do this in a private space so you can be alone with your voice. If you are in a noisy room, head to the bathroom or take a breather outside. If you cannot leave, whisper these words or recite them silently in your head, but make sure your recitation still holds a commanding presence.

MANAGE YOUR EXPECTATIONS

The biggest culprit behind the tendency to be negative may be faulty or skewed expectations. It's difficult to be positive if things never turn out how you expect them to!

For this reason, it's important that you manage your expectations and set realistic goals. If you expect excessively positive outcomes, or positive outcomes in an extremely short period of time, you are setting yourself up for disappointment.

To avoid this disappointment, manage your expectations with the following steps:

1. Think about what you are hoping to achieve, and describe your time frame and desired outcome in detail.

2. Consider whether this outcome is realistic for the average person. Would the average person plucked off the street be able to meet this goal if they were motivated to do so?

3. Consider how much sacrifice this outcome will require. For example, can you give up a little bit of time each day or several hours on the weekend to meet your goal? Or would achieving the goal require several hours a day?

4. Think about whether achieving your desired goal will truly lead to the outcome you expect. If your goal is specific to one area of life, such as your work, are you expecting it to also have a large, positive impact on other areas of your life?

This exercise might seem like a buzzkill, but it's vital to have realistic expectations if you hope to maintain your optimism and not burn yourself out.

SHARE SOMETHING YOU ARE PROUD OF

You've done something great? Share it! You don't exactly need to brag about yourself, as nobody likes a show-off, but sharing an accomplishment or something you're proud of with someone close to you, like a friend or family member, can energize your mind, provide a lift in happiness, and get you out of a burnout slump.

So send a text or call someone to share good news. Since this person cares for you, he or she will probably just be thrilled for you and your success! Think about a few different areas where you excel—they can be big or small. Maybe some of your accomplishments will be small, but they still hold enough importance to brighten your day. For example:

- Your accomplishment could be related to work—perhaps you finished a grueling assignment or impressed your boss at a meeting.
- Your accomplishment could be something silly and fun— maybe you reached your highest score in a word game or finally learned how to cook pasta the way you like.
- Your accomplishment could be related to your personal relationships—maybe you successfully matched two single friends who really hit it off over dinner.

Use your imagination, and don't be afraid to share your good news! You will get a boost of confidence that will spur positive feelings and break the burnout cycle.

FIND THREE GOOD THINGS

An old staple of the positive psychology and self-help movements, this exercise is a tried-and-true way of boosting your sense of gratitude. When you are in the throes of burnout, you tend to look only at the negative side of life. This exercise will help you shift that perspective.

As you go about your day, keep your eyes and ears peeled for any good things that happen to you. It can be all too easy to ignore all the positive things that happen and focus only on the negative things you encounter or experience, so it might take some practice—but don't give up!

At the end of the day, write down three good things that happened to you or around you on that day. They can be small things, like finding a $10 bill in your pocket, or big things, like sharing a romantic new experience with your partner.

Once you have identified the three good things, take a few moments to think about why these things happened. Was it due to fate? Luck? Hard work? The kindness of a friend or family member? Write down two or three sentences on why each good thing happened to you.

Spending just a little bit of time at the end of your day to recognize the good in your life can remove the "negative events only" filter that may have taken residence in your mind and refocus your perspective to one of gratitude for the positive things you experience.

SIT IN SILENCE

We often forget how soothing and stress-relieving it can be to simply sit in silence. This is partly because there is so little silence—there's always something buzzing, beeping, or blaring.

To find a little bit of calm, try savoring the silence. Turn off the TV, silence your phone, switch off the radio, and see if you can find a quiet place away from anyone who might interrupt your few moments of peace and quiet.

When it's quiet, just sit for a few minutes. Drink in the silence, let it wash over you, and absorb it. Think about how great it is to hear absolutely nothing!

After a few moments, you might notice that you are more attentive to even the smallest sounds: the soft tick of the clock, the purring of your refrigerator, the small whoosh sound of your heat or air conditioner kicking on. Cultivate gratitude for your sense of hearing and the wonderful things your ears allow you to hear: your child's laughter, your favorite song, the sound of birds chirping on a spring morning.

Keep that mindfulness with you as you go on about your day to stop the symptoms of burnout before they even begin.

VISUALIZE YOUR HAPPY PLACE

There's something so magical about visualization activities, where you use your imagination to transport yourself to a different place, time, or state of mind to increase your happiness and fight the symptoms of burnout. Using your imagination will increase your creativity and connect you with your feelings and thoughts; it is able to shift you away from negative thinking and reenergize your mind in just a matter of seconds.

The place you want to visualize is up to you. Pick a moment, an environment, preferred company, an era—anything that will provide positivity, stimulation, and warmth. Close your eyes for the full effect, and let yourself escape momentarily from reality. Here's how to visualize that happy place:

1. First, find a setting that relaxes you. Is it a beach? A vacation home? A park? The mountains? This happy place will renew you, hitting on all of your senses. Let's use the beach as an example.

2. Feel the sand in your toes—the grainy, rough texture that still somehow feels incredibly soft to the touch.

3. Listen to the waves crashing and the palm trees swaying in the wind. Feel the warm breeze on your face and in your hair.

4. Smell the seawater or maybe a coconut—something tropical that could be in the vicinity.

Once you're in the midst of visualizing your happy place, take a deep breath, open your eyes, and let the happy feelings you're experiencing energize you for the rest of the day.

FOCUS ON THE PRESENT

Due to the increase in stress and frustration, people experiencing burnout tend to grow cynical and negative about the future. Optimists, on the other hand, tend to not dwell too much on the past or get lost in thoughts of the future; they live fully in the present. When you fully engage with the present, you open yourself up to all the good things happening around you.

Follow these steps to turn your focus from the past or future to the present:

1. Check in regularly with your thoughts. Pause wherever you are and whatever you're doing, and scan your thoughts for preoccupation with the past or future.

2. When you've caught yourself in the act, identify the thought and write it down or make a mental note of it.

3. Think about how this thought ties into your current goals, and identify the most relevant goal. Come up with one idea or action you can take right now or in the very near future to move yourself closer to this goal.

For example, if you find yourself thinking about the time you missed an important deadline, you might tie it to your goal of avoiding procrastination. Instead of dwelling on your past misstep, come up with a step you can take today to break yourself of your procrastination habit, such as taking one concrete action on the project with the nearest deadline.

Give yourself reasons to be optimistic, and you'll find it much easier to actually *be* optimistic!

MAKE A TO-DO LIST

Oftentimes burnout can come from a feeling of being over-whelmed and having too many things to do. Stopping to organize those tasks into a visual list that you can look at and check things off of can give you not only a sense of accomplishment but a sense of relief in the organization of all your tasks. It's hard to try to juggle everything in your head, which is why recording some of those swirling thoughts and ideas can do you good.

Grab a pen and a pad of paper or notebook and flip to a fresh sheet of paper. Write "My To-Do List" at the top, and start writing some of those nebulous tasks and half-finished ideas down on paper. However, if you want to really make an impact on your mood and clear your head, try any of these suggestions:

- At the top of your list, include several to-dos you have recently finished and cross them off. This can give you a wonderful sense of accomplishment and confidence in your ability to continue knocking others out.
- After you write them down, organize them according to importance. Put the to-do that is most important to you at the top and the least important one at the bottom.
- Categorize them by domain. Keep your work-related to-dos in one list, your home maintenance/improvement to-dos in another, and your family- and friend-related to-dos in a third list.
- Set a goal to complete each to-do by a certain date and organize them chronologically. That way, you can cross one off and jump directly to the next one.

SMELL SOMETHING GOOD

Your sense of smell is such a powerful tool. More than any other sense, your sense of smell is intimately tied to your memories. When you smell something uniquely associated with a past experience, you are transported back to that experience in an instant—something that simply doesn't happen as quickly or as intensely when you hear an associated sound or see an associated sight.

If burnout has got you feeling worn ragged and you need a little boost of happiness, take advantage of this huge mood influencer by simply smelling something good. It might be a candle, an air freshener, a specific dish, or even a scent that most people wouldn't find pleasant to smell but that is personally meaningful to you, like the smell of engine oil that reminds you of working on a car with your dad or the scent of a specific type of cleaner your grandmother always used.

Having trouble finding a pleasant scent from your past? You can also try one of these scents that have been proven to boost moods:

- Lemon
- Lavender
- Jasmine
- Cinnamon
- Peppermint

Light the candle, spray the air freshener, or find some other way to enjoy the scent for a few minutes. Let your mind wander back to any good memories you have associated with the smell or, if it's simply a smell you enjoy, let yourself soak in the pleasant aroma.

STOP MAKING UNEVEN COMPARISONS

Constant comparison is bound to leave you feeling frustrated and self-conscious. It's also unhealthy and unhelpful to compare yourself with others too much, especially when you are feeling the stress, frustration, and self-doubt of burnout. However, it's not necessarily the act of comparing that is so harmful. It might be that you're making uneven comparisons.

This is a simple but profound truth that has the potential to trigger an "Aha!" moment: When you compare yourself with others, you are often comparing their strengths to your weaknesses. You rarely compare your strengths to their weaknesses, or your strengths to their strengths. Instead, you jump straight to the comparison with the higher disparity and the unfavorable skew.

It is these uneven comparisons that are damaging to your self-confidence and self-esteem, and they are pretty useless to boot. After all, what do you gain by comparing yourself with others on things you struggle with but they excel at? What valuable insight does this give you, beyond reminding you that you have weaknesses and others have strengths? You already know that!

A comparison that could actually produce useful insight would consider your strengths and the strengths of others, or your weaknesses and the weaknesses of others.

Keep this tendency to make uneven comparisons in mind the next time you think about how you measure up to others, and make sure that any comparisons you do make are on more of an even playing field.

START YOUR DAY WITH A GOAL

Setting a goal or positive intention will make a noticeable impact on your well-being, and it can be something small and easy to attain within a short time frame. Starting your day off with a goal in mind can help steer you in the right direction and get you out the door with a sense of motivation and a mission to get that goal accomplished. It will also help you from feeling overburdened about your day—you know precisely what you need to accomplish. This positive intention could be related to a work assignment—perhaps you need to crush a deadline that day or make a great impression during a business meeting with potential clients. It can also be personal, where the goal could be to reconnect with someone over a text message or a phone call, or to get to know someone a bit better.

Whatever the intention, keep it in your mind throughout the day and be sure to write it down, as holding the weight of your intention in your hand can give it even more power and emphasize its urgency. This reminder can go in a notepad, or you can write it on a sticky note to keep in your bag. You can also write it in the notes application on your cell phone to keep track of it and maintain the proper path for the rest of the day.

Having a goal to start your day and then accomplishing it will give you a sense of accomplishment and happiness.

CREATE A HAPPINESS MANTRA

Mantras are similar to affirmations but are not quite the same. Affirmations are positive statements about who you are right here and right now, while mantras are simply words, phrases, or statements that help you stay focused, mindful, and in the right frame of mind.

This mantra is going to empower you to lift yourself out of the symptoms of mental burnout and make each day more positive. To create your own mantra, come up with something you can repeat to yourself during your day. A successful mantra will achieve these things:

- Remind you of your intention to be more positive.
- Be short and sweet.
- Be easy to remember and repeat.
- Make you smile!

Your mantra can be one or two essentially meaningless syllables, or it can be made of words or phrases that are intensely, personally significant to you. Whatever works for you is a good mantra!

When you create your mantra, stay mindful of your intention and pour that intention into it; you want it to be a good reminder to stay open and invite bliss into each moment.

Once you have your mantra ready to go, remember to use it often!

RELIEVE STRESS IN YOUR GUT

When burnout has you feeling off balance, shift heightened levels of stress in your gut with this easy meditation. Emotions and stress are most often held at the third chakra level, between the belly button and the rib cage. Yoga poses that stimulate this chakra and strengthen your core enable you to release emotions, restore balance, and reclaim peace. Here's how to do it:

1. Stand with feet aligned with your shoulders at a distance of about 1 foot apart. Bend your knees slightly.

2. Press your palms together, and raise your arms over your head. Think of your arms and hands working together to levy a blow, as though you are using a hatchet to open a coconut.

3. Exclaim "Ha!" loudly as you heave down your arms and hands in a single, swift movement to release emotional energy. Repeat until you feel emptied and calm.

4. Move to a nearby wall. Lie supine with your legs up the wall, your palms open, and your eyes closed.

5. Breathe away any remaining stress until peace settles upon you.

REMOVE YOURSELF
FROM THE SITUATION

Sometimes all you need to get rid of burnout is to remove yourself from whatever situation you are currently in—even if it's not a particularly bad situation!

If you find yourself lacking joy and feeling stuck in a stagnant situation, whether it's comfortable and familiar or stifling and unpleasant, just remove yourself. It's best if you physically remove yourself from the situation, but you can always practice some meditation or visualization to remove yourself mentally if physically leaving the area isn't an option.

The important part is to get your mind off your current environment and mix things up a bit. Go somewhere else, do something else, think about something else—whatever it takes to get completely removed from the stagnant situation.

Give yourself some bonus points by engaging in something completely new and maybe even a little bit nerve-racking for you, like going to a social club or organization without knowing anyone or trying a brand-new hobby without any background or experience in it.

Be new! Be bold! You'll thank yourself for it later.

SORT YOUR THOUGHTS

When you are feeling burned out, it's easy to get overwhelmed by your thoughts. You have so many thoughts and feelings and sensations running through your head, it's a wonder how you get anything done! If you've been feeling overwhelmed by your thoughts, give organizing your thoughts a try.

You won't need any paper or a writing implement for this, as all the organizing will happen in your mind.

Find a quiet spot and sit in a comfortable seat. Close your eyes, and allow yourself to sink into the present moment. Observe your thoughts as they come and go.

Once you feel fully engaged in the present moment, envision three buckets. Label one "Thoughts," one "Feelings," and the third "Sensations."

As your thoughts arise, consider them and decide which bucket they fit in.

For example, if the thought "I'm still sore from yoga the other day" arises, you would move it to the "Sensations" bucket. If the thought "I'm excited to see the movie tonight" pops up, you would move it to the "Feelings" bucket. If the thought "I wonder how long I've been doing this" comes up, you would move it to the "Thoughts" bucket.

Continue sorting your thoughts for 5 to 10 minutes. This exercise will force you to focus on the present, since it's very difficult to think about the past or future while sorting your current thoughts!

TURN ON YOUR POSITIVE FILTER

Positive filtering is changing your perspective on the things you see around you. Often, when people are feeling burned out, they tend to focus on the negative in things. This exercise is going to help you change that perspective. Of course, you must let in at least some of the negative things around you for safety and health reasons, but many of us get overwhelmed with the negative and forget to let the positive in as well.

To turn on your positive filter, stop whatever you are doing and take a good look around you. Notice at least one positive thing—like the cheerful sunshine, the leaves blowing in the breeze, a smiling mother and child walking down the street, or a picture of your children on the desk in front of you.

If you truly can't find anything positive in your immediate vicinity, put the exercise on pause and try it again in a little while. Eventually you will be able to find *something* positive nearby.

That's it—that's the whole exercise! Of course, doing this just once won't help you build a more positive outlook—you must repeat this practice multiple times a day to cultivate your positive filter and open yourself up to all the good that life has to offer.

PULL YOUR HAIR

Humans have numerous nerve sensations on their heads. During a massage, the head is a prime area for touch, because there's so much stress stored in the mind from anxiety triggers and even just normal thought processes.

However, gently pulling the strands of your hair—and feeling that strain come up from the roots—can relieve some of that tension. That pressure on your head will clear your mind and provide focus and stimulation. Here's the best way to perform the activity:

1. Grab a bunch of hair strands, down deep near the scalp, in each hand.

2. Slowly extend the strands outward, in any direction you prefer.

3. Be gentle, and stop pulling once you start to feel that your hair can't extend any farther. Hold here for a few counts, breathing slowly.

4. Repeat this activity for a few minutes, taking a few different strands in your hands each time. Make your way around your head, pulling in various directions. When you're finished, gently release your hair strands slowly from your hands. The strands of your hair should feel nice and light.

As the head holds so much strain, playing with your hair and the nerves in your scalp will help remove a lot of that burnout tension and create a calm and more relaxed mind.

MAKE A LIST OF WHAT YOU LIKE ABOUT YOURSELF

For this exercise, you're going to come up with a list of things you like about yourself. Identifying what you like about yourself can be hard—especially if burnout is making you feel low—but it's one of the best things you can do for yourself! Grab a piece of paper or a notebook and something to write with and follow these instructions:

1. Think about yourself from the perspective of your partner, your best friend, or a beloved family member. It can be really difficult to find the right balance, but try to come up with neutral and objective thoughts while maintaining a warm and friendly attitude toward yourself. You want to come up with some accurate strengths and features you appreciate about yourself, but you also want to take a kind perspective rather than a completely cold and detached one.

2. Identify at least five things you like about yourself. One or two can be superficial, but try to focus on qualities, traits, and habits. For example, you might list your eyes, your sense of humor, your work ethic, your fashion sense, and your commitment to helping those less fortunate.

3. Think about how much you appreciate friends and family with these good traits, and tell yourself what you would say to cheer them up or make them feel a little more positive about themselves.

FIND A HAPPY MEMORY

Our minds are rich and complex, full of mysterious process-es and unknown connections. Sometimes reaching into your brain and finding a happy memory is all it takes to break you out of burnout depression and get you seeing things in a more positive light.

Here's how to do it:

1. Look around the room you are in and take a brief mental inventory of the objects within it (e.g., table, tablecloth, two chairs, framed photograph, end table, snow globe, lamp).

2. Rack your brain for a good memory that is connected to one of these items. Try to think of something that in-volved a loved one and/or that resulted in shared love and laughter (e.g., when your brother's dog knocked over the lamp at the worst possible moment, or when your friend brought you the snow globe as a meaningful gift).

3. Replay this entire memory in your head from start to finish.

You will likely find a smile on your face as you finish reliv-ing the memory. Enjoy the smile, cherish the memory, and continue on through your day with just a bit more happiness.

GET YOUR PROBLEMS OFF YOUR CHEST

Paradoxically, talking about your problems can actually reduce your stress and boost your happiness, resulting in decreased burnout. Anyone who has had a good therapist can attest to this phenomenon; sometimes you spend the entire session talking about really difficult stuff, but you leave feeling much better than when you came in.

This happiness boost comes from the cathartic experience of getting something difficult or damaging off your chest. You may also benefit from the commiseration, advice, or perspective of the person you are speaking with. So often, we get caught up in our own lives and forget that there are billions of other humans out there who have many of the same problems we have. Talking to someone who can identify with the problems you are having can be a great source of relief, and even those with no relevant experience can offer soothing empathy.

If you are struggling to come up with someone to talk about your problems with, and seeing a therapist is not feasible at the moment, consider chatting with a total stranger. Be on the lookout—on the Internet or in person—for a friendly or easygoing individual, and offer that person a chance to talk out their problems if they are willing to listen to you do the same.

Pouring your heart out to a stranger can be amazingly therapeutic. After all, they have no preconceived notions or judgments about you, and they can approach your situation from a relatively neutral viewpoint. Don't underestimate the wisdom that you may find in a stranger's words!

MAKE PLANS

You may think that making plans might increase the stress of burnout, as you are adding something else to your to-do list. But, on the contrary, making some plans for something fun to do actually builds excitement and joy for what's to come later. If you have fun plans, such as a dinner with friends, a happy hour, or a movie night with the family, you're going to have something to look forward to. When you're eager for the day's agenda, you'll feel energized to get moving out the door!

Here's what to do. Call or text a friend, or chat with your family about meeting up later. Make a plan. If one person is busy, try another. Spend a few minutes connecting with someone who is available and setting something up.

Even if you don't have a specific activity in mind, just get something on the docket. There's plenty of time to figure out the logistics later. Then when you feel the sadness and struggles of burnout starting to creep into your day, you now have something fun and exciting to think about to make the day seem brighter!

COLOR

There has been plenty of research on the benefits of coloring for improving cognitive function and decreasing stress and depression—two classic symptoms of burnout!

Buy an adult coloring book from the store. If you'd rather not go searching for one, you can always go online to download some free coloring sheets. Then grab some crayons or colored pencils, and let your inner child out to play! Color inside the lines, color outside the lines, make it look realistic, or make it as exotic and surreal as you'd like—however you feel like doing it is fine.

As you color, let yourself remember what it felt like to be a kid. Remind yourself of how great it felt to be carefree and full of joy as a default setting. Allow some of that untarnished joy in life to seep into you and fill you up.

Using your creativity and imagination in this way lets your mind act on its curiosity and discover something new. Channeling this fresh stream of energy can carry over into other areas of life—it will affect work performance, create a positive outlook, and improve your ability to think in out-of-the-box ways. Coloring is also a fun activity that will offer the brain a break when your energy levels are getting low.

So take a few minutes to color. It will not only boost your mood; it will also enhance your quality of life and mental focus in the long run.

PAUSE YOUR NEGATIVE THOUGHTS

Inspiration is a powerful motivator as well as a mood-enhancer—it can have a huge impact on how you feel and help pull you out of symptoms of burnout.

For this exercise, you will put your negative thinking on pause and allow yourself to dwell only on the positive.

1. Think about a current problem or challenge in your life. Is there something that feels overwhelming or impossible?

2. Consider your current thoughts about this problem. They're probably along the lines of "There's no way I can..." or "It's too difficult to...."

3. Write down these negative thoughts on a piece of paper with some space on the page in between thoughts.

4. Now try the possibility mindset: Instead of focusing on all the obstacles between you and solving your problem or meeting your goal, think about all of the possibilities that this challenge opens up to you.

5. For each negative thought, run it through the possibility mindset, and write down what comes out on the other side. For example, "There's no way I can figure this out" could become "I have what it takes to find the solution."

6. Do this for each negative thought. Once you have completed each pair, read through them and highlight, underline, or otherwise call attention to the positive thought. This will help you plant the new thought in your mind.

Revisit these positive thoughts when you need inspiration.

CREATE A YES/MEH LIST

There are bound to be a few tasks that are sucking your energy and leading you down the path to burnout, and if you're given the choice to dismiss them, do so! This will allow you to focus on things that uplift you. Here's what to do:

1. Start a list of items or tasks that are enhancing or zapping your energy stores. Put the items that enhance your energy stores in a "Yes" column and the ones that drain your energy in a "Meh" column.

2. Look at the items that are on your Meh list. Maybe it contains things like the need to go grocery shopping and cook dinner. Consider whether you should forgo them and create a Yes item instead. Here, a Yes might be ordering in, getting delivery form a store, or going out to dinner instead and scheduling a grocery store trip for the next day.

3. In addition to swapping Meh items for more Yes items, consider items that are natural Yes aspects of your life already, and look to them to provide energy. For instance, does speaking to your child or spouse on the phone during the day make you feel connected and loved? Then grab your phone and call!

4. Keep swapping Meh tasks for Yes ones, and add them to the ever-growing list.

That said, if a Meh item is work related and essential to your job, there's no way to get around it. However, incorporating actions that might make the task easier, such as listening to music while doing it, could help.

FIND HUMOR IN THE SITUATION

Humor is one of humanity's most effective tools to fight stress and encourage joy. It is at your disposal 24/7, although you may not always realize it.

To battle burnout, find humor when it is least expected. Follow these steps to give it a shot:

1. When you feel like burnout is overtaking you, stop and look around you. It's probably not a particularly wonderful environment if you are feeling stressed, but take in your surroundings anyway.

2. Find something that could be a source of humor. That might be a silly hat someone is wearing, a misspelling of "detail-oriented" in an email, or any other example of irony or humor.

3. Embrace the humor! Laugh at the silly or ironic thing you noticed and move on to the next bit of funny you can find.

The more you practice finding humor in all situations, the more you will be able to cultivate a sense of happiness anywhere, anytime.

SHOW YOURSELF SOME LOVE

Burnout can make you feel a lot of self-doubt. But in order to break yourself out of that, you need to show yourself some love. Loving yourself is the first step along the way to true happiness, because true happiness is only possible if you come from a place of clarity and acceptance about who you are. To open the door to happiness, work on improving your self-love. Give this simple exercise a try to get started.

Wherever you are and whatever you're in the middle of doing, press the metaphorical pause button. Ask yourself how you're feeling right now, in this very moment. Are you feeling happy? Sad? Stressed out? Nothing in particular?

Whatever term describes your current feelings, tell yourself it's okay to feel that way. There's nothing wrong with feeling however you feel. Offer yourself some acceptance, some compassion, and some love. If it helps, give yourself an actual hug to emphasize the love!

Burnout will try to rob you of your self-confidence and self-worth; don't let it! Remind yourself that feeling a particular way does not define who you are. You are wonderful and worthy of love and abundance!

USE POSITIVE REALISM

Having resilience will not only fight burnout by helping you to minimize life's stressors, it will also help you in coming out of a rough patch stronger than you went in. Unsurprisingly, people who are more optimistic tend to have greater resilience. When you expect good things to happen, it's not so hard to bounce back from the occasional obstacle or setback. It works in the other direction too—when you're always bouncing back to new opportunities and picking up lessons learned along the way, it's easy to be optimistic about the future. Because of this relationship between resilience and optimism, one of the best ways to improve one is to boost the other.

Positive realism is one type of optimism that is accessible even to those who are not natural optimists. Positive realists may acknowledge that the worst is possible, but they spend far more energy hoping and planning for the best. Give this mindset a try with the following steps:

1. Think of an upcoming event or occasion that you are worrying about.

2. Consider all the different possible outcomes (e.g., if the event is a date, think about all the different ways it could turn out, from falling madly in love to leaving in disgust).

3. Determine which outcomes are the most likely. Of these most likely outcomes, at least one or two will be positive (e.g., planning a second date, making a new friend).

4. Commit yourself to looking forward to these positive, realistic outcomes.

TAKE YOUR DOG FOR A WALK

Studies have shown that walking a pet can beat burnout by improving your energy levels and making you happier. Since pups especially can run and play with you, you can actually get your heart rate up quite a bit from all that movement and messing around. Give man's best friend some attention and love, allowing the bonding time to energize you and serve as a distraction from other anxiety-provoking thoughts, such as a work deadline or a big upcoming presentation.

This is a time for you to relax and connect with your pet, so ditch your phone, music, and so on and just focus on these moments outside with your friend. Let your senses take in the world around you, notice the sound of rustling leaves, the smell of fresh cut grass, the feeling of sunshine on your skin. Let your dog lead you (within reason) to where he or she wants to go and feel the release of letting go of a bit of control.

If walking your pet is out of reach due to time constraints, try at least playing with him or her for a few minutes outside. The fresh air will boost both of your energy levels. If you don't have a pet of your own, see if you can play with a neighbor's dog or accompany them on a walk. (Your neighbor may actually be grateful for the help!)

CHALLENGE NEGATIVE THOUGHTS

Burnout can lead you to feeling depressed and lacking self-esteem. While it's normal to feel a little down sometimes, the trouble comes when your negative thoughts start repeating and gaining ground in your mind.

One of the best things you can do for your well-being is to scan your thoughts for those that are negative and challenge them.

First, open yourself up to the thoughts going through your head. Once you have identified a negative thought, challenge it by asking yourself these four questions:

1. Is the thought true?

2. Is it even possible to know if it's true?

3. What effects does believing this thought have on me?

4. What are the potential effects of *not* believing this thought?

Your answers to these four questions can guide you to the best way forward. If the thought is not true and is having harmful effects, you can challenge its validity and commit to questioning this thought whenever it arises.

You can use this exercise for every negative thought that pops up (and some overly positive thoughts too).

PAMPER YOURSELF

This is a really open-ended activity, which makes it perfectly suited for customization.

A fabulous way to fight the monotony and stress of burnout is to inject your day with a bit more bliss! This might be something completely different for you, but here are some common activities that many people find help them feel pampered and fabulous:

- Buying a new book you've been wanting to read
- Buying yourself something really delicious for dinner
- Splurging on a new piece of clothing or another item you've had your eye on
- Getting a long massage or a facial
- Treating yourself to a fancy coffee or a sweet treat you rarely indulge in
- Going to see a guilty-pleasure movie

Whatever it is that makes you feel pampered, fabulous, and luxurious—do it! You shouldn't pamper yourself all the time, but make sure you do it at least once in a while to invite more happiness into your life.

CONSIDER THE ROAD NOT TAKEN

Feeling burned out can give you a negative view of the current state of your life, but in this exercise, you'll reflect on your past and find contentment in the choices you made.

Identify the two or three choices that you are the proudest of making, the ones you believe had the most significant impact on your life. These don't necessarily need to be the weightiest decisions—like the decision to propose to your significant other or take a new job across the country—they just need to be important moments in your life. For example, you might choose telling the truth in a moment when it mattered most. Or perhaps you decided to stay home and help take care of a sick relative instead of moving away for an educational or career opportunity, and this decision allowed you to make meaningful connections you otherwise wouldn't have been able to make.

Using your 20/20 hindsight, think about how your life might have turned out if you hadn't taken those risks or made those good decisions. What would have happened if you had lied in that pivotal moment? Where would you be if you had taken that opportunity instead of staying to fulfill your familial responsibilities? Consider where you would be right now, who you would be with, and what you would be doing.

Reflect on all the things that make you happy that you probably wouldn't get to enjoy if you had taken the other road—like your spouse, your current home, a job you enjoy—and find a sense of pride in the decision you did make and the positive impact it has had.

BREAK PROBLEMS INTO SMALLER STEPS

When you are feeling burned out, life's problems may seem bigger and more challenging than usual. Some problems may feel so big that you don't see how you could possibly overcome them. When you are faced with such a problem, one of the best ways to keep yourself upright and moving forward is to break things down into small, meaningful steps.

As an example, imagine your problem is a looming project deadline at work, and you've been procrastinating. The first part of your solution might be putting together an executive summary of your project.

Next is the most important piece—break that part into small, manageable steps. Your first step might be as simple as gathering all your project-related documents. Step two could be to open a blank document and give it a relevant title. In step three, you might create a high-level outline for the summary. Continue until you reach the end of your solution.

When you have all of your steps planned, the problem likely won't seem quite so large anymore. Practice stepping through your problems to build inner resilience and face your future challenges with greater confidence in your ability to overcome!

GET EXCITED ABOUT SOMETHING

Excitement, as an emotion, creates momentum, stimulating both the mind and body at the same time. So if you're stuck in a burned out mindset, think of something that you're looking forward to for that instant pick-me-up! When you imagine life's greatest adventures and gifts, and think about how they can affect your life, it's hard not to get happier about what's in store. For example:

- Do you have a vacation approaching?
- Are you looking forward to a special occasion, such as an anniversary or a child's birthday?
- Are you in the running for a big promotion at work and can already taste the flavors of that congratulatory cake?
- Do you have plans to catch up with a friend you haven't seen in a while?
- Are you planning to sign up for a new workout class you've wanted to challenge yourself with?
- Is your child in an upcoming school play or recital that you're looking forward to seeing?
- Are you meeting someone for a date who has been fun to chat with over the phone?

Focusing on this event for just a few minutes will provide long-lasting benefits, and you'll have an excited smile on your face for hours after.

FIND PEACE WITH DEEP BREATHING

When you are feeling the stress of burnout, try this simple exercise to find some calm.

1. Sit down in a comfortable chair or on the floor. Get comfortable, but not too comfortable. Sit with a straight back and rest your hands on your lap, or place one hand on your chest and the other on your stomach. Close your eyes and just sit for a moment, getting accustomed to how you feel in this position.

2. Take a deep breath in through your mouth or your nose, hold it in your lungs for 1 second, then exhale deeply. You should fill your lungs completely on the in breath and empty them completely on the out breath.

3. During each breath, pay attention to the feeling of fullness in your chest and the ensuing emptiness when you expel the air. If you have one hand on your chest and the other on your belly, feel the slow, steady rise and fall as you breathe.

4. Continue breathing with this method for 3 minutes or at least twenty breaths.

5. Once you have finished your deep breathing, think about how you feel now compared with before you began the exercise. Don't be surprised if you feel calmer and more collected after the breaths—this is a common reaction!

You can use this simple well-being exercise anytime, but keep it in mind especially for situations in which you need to find peace or create calm within yourself.

PREP FOR TOMORROW

Nothing can make you more tired and burned out than thinking about what a stressful day you have ahead of you come morning. So take a few minutes once you're home in the evening to plan out the following day, jotting down everything you need to accomplish and providing steps for how best to find success and manage your time. Making a list is a great way to improve your energy, as it gets you thinking in a productive manner. Knowing that you have a set list of things to do and a clear direction in mind for the following day will help you feel less stressed, so you can enjoy your current evening with newfound energy.

If you need to prioritize what you need to get done, write that down. If there's a morning errand you need to do in order to prepare for something later in the day, take note of that as well, and consider whether you might need to shift things around in the morning—take your breakfast to go or set the alarm earlier. Soon, you'll feel less stressed and have the energy to really enjoy your evening, knowing that you'll have a plan set for the next day.

IDENTIFY YOUR GOALS

Having a set of goals that are achievable and meaningful to you can help carry you through the tough times. It's easier to persevere and bounce back when you have a desirable goal to motivate you!

You probably already know the benefits of having smart professional goals, but it can be difficult to come up with your own personal, meaningful goals. If you've struggled to identify your goals, try these steps:

1. Identify what is most important to you. Think about what your values are, what your desires for your future are, and what makes you happiest. Write these things down in a notebook or journal.

2. Narrow this list to the most important three or four things. If you need help narrowing down, think about which things you feel you can't live without.

3. For each important thing, imagine what your life would look like if you put this front and center. Write a few sentences about how you'd like to incorporate or live out this value in your life.

4. Read over what you wrote for each important thing and distill the paragraph into a one-sentence goal with a specific, achievable outcome.

Congratulations, you've identified your life goals!

MAKE MINDFUL TRANSITIONS

With the ultra-packed schedules and multiple commitments of life today, it can be tempting to rush straight from one task or activity to the next. When you have a million things to get done, it's hard to justify taking even the smallest break. However, this approach leads to distraction, stress, and burnout, making you ultimately less effective.

By spending just a few moments shifting your mindset from one task to the next, you can improve your mindfulness and improve your efficiency.

Commit to trying this technique for one whole day. Each time you find yourself about to switch from one task to the next (e.g., from parking at work to preparing to start your workday, moving from finishing up a report to working on a spreadsheet), follow these steps:

1. Pause, even if you're in a hurry. It will only take a few moments!

2. Mentally confirm that you are done with the task you were just doing. Put it completely aside.

3. Focus on your breathing for five breaths. If your breathing is rapid or irregular, try counting to five on the inhale, pausing for 2 seconds, counting to five on the exhale, and pausing for 2 seconds again.

4. Mentally shift gears to the task you are about to start.

This extremely simple exercise can have a big impact on how calm and focused you feel, and it only takes a few minutes!

TREAT THIS DAY AS IF IT WERE YOUR LAST

How often do you notice your mood getting worse because of little things, like traffic or a minor disagreement with your significant other? It probably happens more often than you'd like, and this negative outlook can put you on the fast track to burnout. It's surprisingly easy to let little things drag you down. Luckily, it's also fairly easy to put them in perspective.

This exercise is based on a pretty popular idea of shifting your perspective from the small and ultimately insignificant things to the broader picture.

When you find yourself bogged down in all the little things that have gone wrong in your day, stop and ask yourself two questions:

1. What if today were the last day of my life?

2. How would I want to spend my day if it were my last?

These two simple questions have the extraordinary power to pull you out of your temporary bad mood and take you to the 30,000-foot view of your life. From this perspective, even the things that made you the angriest or most irritated during the day become no bigger than specks, not even worth mentioning.

However, the truly good things will remain as big as ever. Imagining today as your last day will help you to put aside minor annoyances and focus on the positive things you value most.

Chapter 4

REFUEL
YOUR
EMOTIONS

Burnout can take a toll on your emotions, leaving you feeling trapped or stuck in your life and making you feel like everything is going wrong. When you are emotionally exhausted, you lose your enthusiasm for things in your life, you feel empty and drained of emotion and stretched too thin. Fortunately, there are ways to reverse the emotional drain of burnout and find renewed appreciation for your life and the things in it.

The exercises in this chapter will help you deal with your emotions (whether they be positive or negative), will help you express and acknowledge those emotions to yourself and others, and will help you work on seeing life in more positive terms. You'll find feel-good activities and exercises that can help you cut down the negativity of burnout before it overwhelms you. These exercises will safeguard your emotions from the toll of burnout and help lift you out when you are feeling low.

BE YOUR OWN CHEERLEADER

When you are feeling like you're spent and don't have anything left to give, affirmations will give you that much needed boost of energy, motivation, and happiness. Taking just a few minutes to reaffirm that you are a good person can make all the difference in how you feel about yourself.

First, you'll need to come up with some affirmations. Follow these easy guidelines:

1. Make your affirmation short and sweet; it shouldn't be longer than one short sentence, and it should focus on just one idea (e.g., "I am a good person," not "I am a good person who is talented at basketball, skillful in my craft, and an excellent father").

2. Make sure It Is worded in the here and now—in this exact moment, at this very spot.

3. Make it a positive statement about yourself that represents what you want to be, what you hope to be, and what you know you are capable of in the near future.

Here are a few examples to help you get started:

- I am a kind and generous person.
- I have valuable talents and skills to offer.
- I am a good [daughter, sister, friend, spouse, or mother].

Once you have a list of a few positive, present-tense, and uplifting affirmations, it's time to start practicing! Repeat them right away and then plan out a few periods throughout your day when you can repeat them again. Once you do, you'll feel an instant boost of positive energy!

PUT ON YOUR FAVORITE OUTFIT

When you need a quick boost to your self-confidence or self-esteem during the throes of burnout, doing something as simple as trying on your favorite outfit can help.

Your favorite outfit is your favorite for a reason—it makes you look good and feel good about yourself. In some cases, it can even act as a sort of mask or costume, helping you to put on the persona of someone who is more confident, someone more self-assured, or someone who seems exceedingly capable.

Drag your favorite pieces out of your closet and slip into them. Stand in front of the mirror in your best outfit and drink in the view. Let the confidence and self-esteem seep in, and enjoy the boost to your self-assurance and body bliss!

Use this exercise to remind you of how it feels to have confidence in yourself and to remind yourself that you have the capacity to feel like that all the time. Your mind is the only thing holding you back!

CHALLENGE YOUR INNER CRITIC

When you are burned out, it can often seem like you can't do anything right. You may feel like everything you try fails, and the negative self-talk can start to overwhelm you. To battle this self-sabotage, one of the best things you can do for yourself is to get a hold of your inner critic. We all have one—that small voice in the back of your mind that plays off your worst anxieties, causing you to question your worth.

You don't need to completely silence this nitpicky voice; you just need to know when to listen to it and when (and how) to tell it to shut up. This exercise is best practiced when your inner critic is loud and obnoxious, since that's when it's easy to catch. When your inner critic pops up, try this:

1. Identify the things your inner critic is saying and the things that are coming from the authentic "you."

2. Take what the inner critic says under advisement; consider whether it's right in any respects or if it's way off base this time. If it helps, feel free to make a list, write in your journal, or take some notes.

3. Address your inner critic gently and compassionately. Try saying, "Inner Critic, I know you're worried about X, but you really don't need to be. Here's my plan for dealing with X....We're going to be fine."

Remember, your inner critic is a part of you, and though it is often misguided, it's trying to look out for your best interests. Treat it with care, and you'll see it begin to soften.

LEARN SOMETHING NEW

There are so many potential benefits to learning new things. Beyond the obvious advantage of building your knowledge, learning something new can also open you up to fresh and exciting opportunities, give you a rush of feel-good chemicals, and improve your self-confidence and self-esteem.

Cultivating a learning mindset is a great way to bolster your well-being and fight burnout, and it's surprisingly easy to do. Simply dedicate yourself to learning one new thing every day.

The new thing could be experimenting with a recipe you've never tried before, researching a fun fact about your favorite historical figure, or watching a how-to video on a craft or activity you'd like to try. You could also go for a more involved learning experience by signing up for a class on a new language, a course in a topic outside of your area of expertise, or lessons in playing a musical instrument.

Whether you choose to learn a one-time fact or to develop a long-term skill, you will reap the benefits from learning every day. Building and enhancing your love of learning will keep you open to new experiences and new knowledge, something that is invaluable in our rapidly changing world.

You can award yourself bonus "well-being points" for learning something new from a friend, acquaintance, or friendly stranger. When you learn interesting new things from someone, you associate those things with that person, making it easy to lay the foundations for a new friendship or to build up an existing one.

PRACTICE FORGIVENESS

One of the best things you can do for your own sense of optimism is to let go of old disappointments and grudges. Extending forgiveness to those people who have wronged you is not really a generous act for them, it's a generous act for yourself!

Instead of carrying around all the wrongs done to you as emotional baggage—which can weigh you down and increase your feelings of sadness and burnout—try forgiving the transgressors and letting the hurt go.

To practice this liberating and uplifting exercise, first identify an old wound you are still nursing. Note what happened, who wronged you, and what the fallout over the incident was. Accept that these are the facts and that nothing can change them.

Next, think about how the experience changed you. It may have made you more cautious and less willing to be vulnerable, but it may have also taught you something important about yourself. Note any positive growth that occurred.

Think about the person who hurt you. Remind yourself that they are human and therefore makes mistakes, just like you. Imagine yourself in their shoes and come up with a scenario in which you may have taken the same action.

Write your words of forgiveness down or say them out loud: "[Person's name], I forgive you for [the wrong]."

This exercise will help you identify a grudge, acknowledge any good that came of it, empathize with the other person, and put the hurt behind you.

PLAY YOUR FAVORITE SONG

When burnout has you feeling fatigued and melancholy, you need to find ways—even if they are just small things—to put a smile on your face and give you motivation to keep going. Music is one of those things that can help. Music is such a wonderful tool for influencing your mood and shaping your experiences. Use this exercise to remind yourself just how powerful music really is.

Find a quiet spot or pull out your headphones if you're in a public place. Find one of your favorite songs—preferably one with an upbeat tone—and start listening. As you listen to this much-loved song, think about three things:

1. How grateful you are for the ability to listen to music (if you are deaf or hard of hearing, read the lyrics to your favorite song or poem instead).

2. What this song brings up in your mind—a specific memory or perhaps a daydream or fantasy? Does it make you remember good times or look forward to new ones?

3. What the artists might have been thinking and feeling when they created this piece of art for you and all their other listeners.

Take time to appreciate the music, and you'll get a nice little boost of happiness and beat some of the burnout blues!

TRY EARLY MORNING JOURNALING

Feeling burned out can lead to a lack of motivation and general malaise. When these feelings make it hard for you to get your day going, try an early morning journaling session. Some of the benefits of journaling in the morning include:

- Starting the day on a positive note. Try writing about something you are grateful for each morning, and you'll notice that this sense of gratitude makes your day a little brighter.
- Aligning yourself with your goals. Writing about your goals and dreams each morning helps keep you focused on those goals all day long.
- Focusing your mind and helping you get rid of the clutter. Writing down all your thoughts in the morning helps get them out of your mind and allows you to be able to focus on the important things.

Give morning journaling a try by following these guidelines:

- Focus on the day ahead. With a morning journal session, you will spend most of your time thinking about the day to come.
- Write about what you expect will happen today. Do you have anything in particular coming up today? A presentation at work, a date night, or an important meeting?
- Write about what you hope will happen today. How do you want that presentation, date night, or meeting to go?

By focusing on the near future, some realistic outcomes, and some hoped-for outcomes, you will get some good practice being more forward-looking and optimistic but still realistic.

INDULGE A LITTLE

Life is about balance—and that means you should be able to energize yourself by indulging in something special every day. Make it small—a video clip that makes you laugh, a few spritzes of perfume, a bite or two of your favorite food—then change it up and relish in the moments. Yes, that means you can and should make room for desserts and salty snacks. In fact, when it comes to dieting, having an 80/20 lifestyle— where you eat clean for 80 percent of the time and enjoy sweets and "less healthy" foods for the other 20 percent of the time—has been shown to provide the greatest benefits and staying power.

When you restrict yourself from life's pleasures, you run the risk of burnout, where you might act out in the opposite manner and sabotage your positive intentions. This vicious cycle increases feelings of depression, anxiety, and resentment, so make it a point to take a few minutes each day to do something just for you! Try anything that makes you feel special, alive, and not deprived one bit!

CELEBRATE THE SUCCESS OF OTHERS

Aside from improving your relationships with others, being positive and congratulatory when someone else succeeds benefits you as well. When you spend time cultivating an attitude of appreciating success, no matter who it is that's enjoying that success, you will find that success comes more easily to you too.

The next time you are feeling burned out and down about or envious of another's success, try this technique to bring yourself out of your funk and encourage yourself to think optimistically:

1. Think about how much time and effort that person put into their success. Generally, achievements and accolades don't just fall into your lap—you have to work for them.

2. Next, imagine how this person is feeling about their success. Visualize their sense of joy, accomplishment, and pride.

3. Put yourself in their shoes. Imagine you are experiencing this success, and open yourself up to the same feelings of joy, accomplishment, and pride. Revel in this feeling of success.

4. Remind yourself that their success is not related to yours. Their success doesn't make your future success any less likely.

5. Wrap all of these thoughts and feelings up into a sense of pride and happiness for the other person. Commit to congratulate them and to mean it when you say it.

LOOK AT OLD PHOTOS

As we grow older, we tend to forget that we've done quite a bit of growing and changing. Acknowledging that the only constant is change can help you to better understand yourself and your journey, to boost your appreciation for everything you have, and to simply be happier and healthier!

If this sounds like a good idea for you, all you need to do is pull out some old photo albums. Spend a few minutes looking back at yourself at several different ages. If you have baby pictures, check out a couple of those. See if you can find some old elementary school and middle school pictures, and check to see if you have any yearbooks from high school.

Look at photos from your childhood all the way up to the last few years and think about how much you have changed. Think about the knowledge, skills, and experience you have now.

Finish off this exercise by taking a picture of yourself right now. Now you'll have a new picture to add to your time line!

MAKE SOMEONE LAUGH

There's no greater gift than laughter, and both you and the one you make laugh will feel a boost of happiness and energy. You'll be battling burnout for both of you! How does laughter boost energy? Well, it instantly alerts you to your current situation, and it elicits an enthusiastic response in the form of a laugh. It also lowers the stress hormone cortisol, which has been shown to zap energy and increase negativity.

Plus, if something's really funny and you can't help but giggle, it's a welcome break from the burnout that has been draining your energy stores. Of course, laughter comes in all forms, so go with whatever you think fits based on the recipient's personality or whatever the moment brings.

You could share a humorous story about your day, tell a joke (a good dad joke never hurts), or share a funny link or meme on the Internet through social media. In any case, knowing that you've put a grin on someone else's face will plant an equally bright one on yours as well, and you'll notice your energy go way up.

EXERCISE YOUR CREATIVITY

One of the symptoms of burnout is a lack of creativity and new ideas. If this is you, don't fear. It can be easy to get back that feeling of happiness that creativity brings, you just need to give yourself a little push.

Doing something creative can be an excellent boost to your well-being. It feels good to apply your skills, stretch your abilities, and make something new and original.

This exercise is great, because it is so customizable. Are you interested in writing fiction? Put pen to paper and write one chapter, or even just a few pages!

Do you love poetry? Pen a poem.

Are you passionate about graphic design? Create a logo that expresses who you are today, at this very moment.

Is cooking your passion? Take an old standby recipe, and challenge yourself to add at least three new ingredients to totally transform the dish.

The point of this exercise isn't to create something that will win awards or sell books, but to give your creative side a chance to express itself. Don't worry if your creation isn't objectively good. Instead, focus on how it makes you feel.

Whenever you need a pick-me-up, switch up your routine by doing something creative. You won't regret it!

WINK AT YOURSELF

This activity might sound silly, but it's foolproof! Winking builds confidence, as it's a sensation that can make you feel sexy, in control, and alive—all of which can reshape your whole mental state for a positive day ahead and keep burnout at bay. So look in the mirror and give yourself a good wink. You can even add on to this by saying, "Hey there, good looking" or "You're looking like a star today." It's a great way to feel good about yourself and get yourself eager to get outdoors and let your radiance shine. Plus, it's quick and easy to do—you don't need to stare at yourself winking for hours in order to get the benefits.

If you feel embarrassed, do this in private. That means if your spouse, child, or coworker is sharing a bathroom with you, hold off. Wait for that person to exit and then compliment yourself, however you may choose. Just remember that there's nothing to be embarrassed about here—you deserve to acknowledge how awesome you are!

TAKE A HIGHER VIEW

When you feel burned out, you have a tendency to get bogged down with minor annoyances. This is a natural tendency, but one that is not very helpful! Sometimes all you need to do to improve your well-being is to change your perspective. Pull out this exercise when something has you feeling down, upset, or irritated.

1. Identify what is dragging down your mood. Be honest with yourself and avoid self-judgment. Hold the source of your annoyance in your mind, and visualize it in detail if that helps you.

2. Next, imagine getting into a helicopter (metaphorical or physical) and slowly lifting off from the thing that is dragging you down. Watch as it gets smaller and smaller.

3. Once you can hardly see it anymore, look up and around you. What do you see? What is at this higher level of attention?

If your irritation is bad drivers in traffic, taking the helicopter view can show you that there are hundreds or even thousands of people just like you who are also feeling the same aggravation right now. When you look up, you'll see the big picture: You'll be home sooner or later, and by next week, you'll have forgotten all about this irritation.

You can try this for any problem, big or small, silly or serious. There is always a higher view you can take to bring some perspective to your problems.

TELL SOMEONE WHAT YOU LOVE ABOUT HIM OR HER

Gratitude and love bring vivacity and energy to your life. They likely remind you of human connection and how meaningful this connection is to your health and happiness. On the opposite side, isolation and loneliness can lead to burnout and depression, which will zap you of motivation and strength.

Take a few minutes today and single out one person who holds great value in your heart. Write an email, send a letter, send a text message, or actually call your friend or family member to share just how much you care and recognize his or her positive qualities. Touch on a few examples. Is this person reliable? Trustworthy? Fun to be around? Does he or she have a good sense of humor and can make you laugh easily? Is he or she selfless, always looking out for your well-being? Share your appreciation to brighten his or her day as well as yours.

TALK TO A STRANGER

Conversation, by itself, is stimulating to the mind, but when it comes to one with someone you haven't met before, the novelty of the situation makes it even more interesting. It's the easiest way to get a quick boost to your mood and energy, as you can find a stranger anywhere. Whether you are simply asking for directions or a recommendation for a great place to grab a bite, or whether you stop someone on the street to pay a compliment or inquire where he or she purchased a bag or shirt, it doesn't take much effort, and it'll lead to some sort of light discussion.

Plus, human connection in general has been shown to improve energy and mood and improve your feeling of well-being, so this type of interaction is a no-brainer when it comes to brain-boosting benefits. If you're shy, start by approaching people you work with or know but haven't spoken to very often. It's a good starting point toward working your way up to meeting a stranger.

MAKE A FUN PURCHASE

Retail therapy is *not* a good long-term option for enhancing your happiness, but a small, well-deserved gift for yourself every now and then can help lift you out of the lows of burnout and give you a boost of joy.

Think about something you really want—not something you need, just something you want. It should be something fun, unnecessary, and not too terribly expensive. Think about a fancy new pillow, a kitchen accessory, or a tool that will make your life just a little bit easier. Try to align it with your values and interests (e.g., go for the kitchen accessory if you're a big foodie or an avid recipe experimenter).

Once you have figured out what you want to treat yourself with, you have two options:

1. Find out where this item is sold and plan when you'll go buy it.

2. Find this item online and order it from your phone or laptop.

Option 1 is the better one, because you get to make a whole experience out of treating yourself, but Option 2 can be super convenient if the store that sells it is far away or if its hours do not match your schedule.

Whichever option you take, enjoy your fun new purchase!

LIST YOUR STRENGTHS

A good way to combat burnout is to work on feeling better about yourself. It's much easier to feel productive and joyful when you feel good about yourself! If you have trouble feeling good about yourself, try directing your attention toward the best parts of you. Follow these easy steps to get on your way to a happier you:

1. First, grab a pen and a piece of paper so that you can record your strengths instead of just thinking about them in the moment.

2. Next, think about activities and tasks or chores that you do well, that you enjoy, and/or that you receive compliments on, and jot these down. Remember, there may be a lot of things that you are good at but hate doing. These are not strengths. A strength should be something that you have a passion or desire to do, something that makes you feel happy and strong inside.

3. Take a moment to think about what it is that makes you good at these things, and write that trait or quality down. For example, if you find yourself finishing crossword puzzles in no time at all, then you might note that you are a good problem-solver or that you have a knack for language.

And voilà! You have a list of your strengths that you can refer to when you want to feel a little happier with yourself.

TRY A NEW HOBBY

Have you wanted to learn to sew? Make a chocolate soufflé? Play the piano? Become fluent in a foreign language? Try stand-up comedy or improv? Nothing bursts the burnout bubble of stagnation like a new hobby to give your life an energizing purpose.

As long as you practice your new skill each day, you will make progress over time, and pretty soon you'll be showing off your new talent to those around you! It might seem scary to try something new—especially when you might be pretty bad at it to start—but as long as you stay committed and enthusiastic, you'll naturally improve.

Still, no matter how masterful you become, each time you practice your new hobby, your mood will benefit. Studies show that doing something you're passionate about can drastically enhance well-being and drive. Use your new hobby as something to look forward to after a long day at work or as soon as you open your eyes in the morning.

Learning a new hobby is a great way to help you feel connected to the world in those unusual, personal ways that make you who you are!

TRY THE THREE-TO-ONE RULE

The three-to-one rule is a method for noticing and identifying at least three positive things for every one negative thing around you. Sometimes this exercise is easy and sometimes it's not, but you'll find it gets easier the more you practice it. You'll also find yourself feeling less burned out as you shift your focus toward the positive.

Here's how to give the three-to-one rule a try:

1. Look around and identify the first negative thing that comes to mind (e.g., a dirty house, a rude customer, an annoying coworker).

2. Now look around and identify three positive things to counteract the one negative (e.g., the many pictures of your happy family on the fridge, three smiling customers, or three nice emails you have received).

3. Continue this process until you've found three good things for each negative thing you notice in the room.

Practicing the skill of finding three times the good relative to the bad will make you a more positive person overall and more naturally attuned to the positive, which can make life seem happier as well.

TUCK YOURSELF IN WITH AFFIRMATIONS

If the stress of burnout is making it tough to sleep, try some nighttime affirmations to help prepare for a peaceful and restful night. When you're getting ready for bed, take a few minutes to stand in front of the mirror and repeat your affirmations to your reflection. Make sure to:

1. Look yourself in the eyes.

2. Say your affirmations out loud.

3. Believe them!

That last part might take some practice, but that's why we say affirmations more than once.

Here are some examples:

- I release the worry, fear, and anxiety of today, and my mind is calm.
- I am grateful for today and the lessons it has brought.
- I have done my best today and earned this rest.
- I am happy with what I have accomplished today.
- I am looking forward to tomorrow and the opportunities it brings.
- I can rest deeply and fully and awake refreshed.

When you're finished, hop into bed and repeat them once more, either aloud or in your head. If you can, use them as a sort of lullaby to drift off to sleep. Going to bed with positive, happy thoughts will lead to positive, happy dreams and a better outlook in the morning.

RELINQUISH THE NEED TO CONTROL

With this guided meditation, you will discover how much easier life can be when you set an intention and let go of the need to control how and when it comes. The stress of needing to control things in your life will wear heavily on your body and mind, and simply letting some of that control go will bring you a sense of lightness and peace. Here's how to do it:

1. Keep your breathing natural.

2. Still the chatter in your mind by linking a numerical count to each inhalation and the words "I am" to each exhalation, and repeat until you feel relaxed and your mind is quiet.

3. Mentally declare your intention—be brief and specific, stating your desire in a positive rather than a negative declaration. For example, avoid saying something like, "I don't want to hear bad news about my recent job interview." Instead, say, "I nailed my job interview and welcome the manager's call to tell me, 'You're hired!'"

4. Trust that the universe has received your intention declaration and is responding in kind.

5. Embrace infinite possibilities as you let go and remember the old adage, "Each thing comes in its own perfect time."

BE OPEN TO LOVE

It can be hard to let love in—there's a natural fear in people when it comes to getting close to someone new, being vulnerable, and accepting that things might not work out. However, if you can put those anxieties aside and be open to affection and warmth, the rewards will bring a remarkable boost of happiness.

Love comes in many forms: love from yourself, family, friends, a significant other, and even a pet. Figure out the areas where you need more love in your life, and work toward making connections that can fill that void. Devote a few minutes each day to engage in this love, and build on it. Here are some ideas:

- Give someone you love a quick embrace. If it's a partner, give a kiss on the lips, cheek, or forehead. If it's a friend, try a hug or a pat on the back.
- Take 5 minutes to play with your pet or to watch a cute video of a pet online.
- Video chat with a relative or friend living in another city for a quick catch-up.
- Spontaneously ask your partner for a date night to deepen your relationship.
- Doodle a few symbols of love, such as a heart or lips. The images will make you feel more open to love.
- Look at a photo of a moment when you were in love, whether it's with a hobby or a person.
- Write down three things you love about the world and three things you'd like to fall in love with in the future.

Let love work its powers and bring meaning and hope to your life.

STARGAZE

Sometimes stepping away from life and getting lost in the wonder of nature can help you feel more connected to the world and battle the loneliness and sadness of burnout. A great way to do this is to stare at the stars.

Wait until the sky is as dark as it gets in your area—or better yet, take a short trip to somewhere with an even clearer view. Then lay down a blanket, set up a chair, or simply stand and stare straight up at the sky.

Look at all the stars and think about how many more stars there are that you simply can't see. Take a moment to appreciate the vastness of the universe and imagine how many other solar systems and planets like ours are out there.

As you revel in the beauty of the stars, try this quick meditation:

- Relax your body and close your eyes for a moment.
- When you open them back up, try to take in the vastness of the night sky. Let your vision be broad and look at the stars without thinking of them specifically or any preconceived notions you have about them, like which ones make up which constellations. Instead, just be open to the vastness of the sky and the universe.
- Think about how lucky you are to be where you are, when you are, and how you are, being able to look up at the sky and engage your imagination.
- Let the stars make you feel small and slight, and revel in the feeling that you are a tiny part of something so much bigger than you.

KEEP A FUTURE DIARY

In times of burnout ruled by doubt, disappointment, or pessimism, it can often be helpful to envision a positive future. In addition to soothing your fears and helping you open yourself up to possibility, this can be a great way to encourage yourself to strive toward a challenging goal. If you don't have a specific goal in mind at the moment, focus on a future in which you have found solutions to your biggest current problems.

Follow these steps to write your future diary entry:

1. Grab your journal, notebook, or diary (or even just a scrap of paper), and something to write with.

2. Give your entry a date that represents when you believe your goal may be accomplished or near completion.

3. Imagine yourself at this date and reflect on how you will feel. Consider how your life—including your work, relationships, and overall lifestyle—will have changed between now and then.

4. Write your diary entry for this future date, focusing on the progress you made to get there and the ways your life has improved since the present.

Visualizing a positive future in which you are nearing your goals or enjoying the fruits of your labor can boost your motivation, your optimism and self-confidence, and your current happiness.

LOOK FOR THE SILVER LINING

One of the ways in which resilient people differ from the not-so-resilient is in their ability to see the positive in any situation, also known as *finding the silver lining*. Those high in resilience tend to search for the positive when they face a struggle rather than wallowing in the negative. To build your resilience, practice finding the silver lining.

The next time you are faced with a challenging, upsetting, or painful situation, find a quiet moment to sit and think. Come up with at least one positive outcome or side effect of your situation. It may take you a while, but don't give up! Something will eventually come to you.

The silver lining could be a new door of possibility opening up when a much-desired one closes. It could be that a positive thing happens to someone else as a result of your situation. If there is really no direct positive effect, then perhaps the silver lining is that you will come out the other side stronger and wiser.

Once you become adept at finding the silver lining, you can aim to come up with a balance of positive and negative effects instead of one solitary good thing. In other words, for every negative aspect of a situation, you could acknowledge that it *is* painful or difficult—but note that something good comes out of it as well.

Practice finding the silver lining and you will find yourself well on the way to battling burnout!

DON'T SWEAT THE SMALL STUFF

If you freak out over every setback or worry, you'll start to feel drained, it'll be hard to break out of that negative mood, and you will put yourself on the path to burnout. While there are certain things in life that are worth fretting about— losing your job, moving to a new city, or missing an important event—smaller, more trivial obstacles shouldn't hold too much weight, so don't let them drive you crazy! Instead, take a few minutes to acknowledge that a minor mistake is okay— you will overcome it.

Consider who it affected, what the actual worst outcome could be, and what you really think is going to happen before you get too unsettled. Also, think rationally—is there a way you can fix the problem? How can you make up for the mistake? By thinking with a sense of calm and having a determined attitude, you'll feel energized and empowered to stand strong and make things right, rather than getting too caught up in the worries and negativity of it all.

BE GRATEFUL

Burnout can give you a negative view on your life, but if you take the time to find gratitude for things in your life, no matter how big or small, you will find you become happier and more positive. Notice and give thanks for simple blessings—the ability to breathe in and out without effort, to taste the sweetness of your favorite dessert, to smell a flower, to feel the breeze against your skin, to hear the wind in the trees, and to see a shooting star. Notice these things in the moment. Feel a genuine appreciation in the core of your being by trying these steps:

1. Calm your mind and sit quietly.

2. Take stock of what you have in your life. For example:
   - An able, strong body
   - A healthy mind
   - Love of family and friends

3. Work through each bulleted item on this list (or one you create) by affirming each item: "I am blessed with a strong body." Feel genuine appreciation for your body.

4. Affirm your gratitude: "For a strong body, I give thanks."

5. Go the next item and assert: "I am blessed with a healthy mind."

6. Continue as before in the same pattern until you've worked your way through all the items.

PUT YOURSELF IN AN UNCOMFORTABLE SITUATION

Yes, it sounds counterintuitive! But the fact is that difficult, challenging, and uncomfortable situations are the only situations in which you grow, and you often find that happiness is tied to personal growth. When you are feeling burned out, you may look at life as stagnant and a drudgery, but growing personally can change that.

To give yourself more opportunities for personal growth, make it a point to put yourself in a brief uncomfortable situation. Here are some suggestions if you're not sure where to start:

- Sign up to attend a networking event where you don't know anybody.
- Volunteer to present something important and complex at work.
- Ask someone to teach you something you have absolutely no understanding of.
- Introduce yourself to a stranger for no reason other than to get to know a stranger!

These are just a few of the many examples of situations that are uncomfortable for many people. If none of these sounds particularly uncomfortable, come up with your own uncomfortable scenarios and seek them out.

It will be hard, but remind yourself that this is the only way to grow, and personal growth leads directly to greater bliss.

TRY SUNSET MINDFULNESS

When you are feeling burned out, it can be hard to appreciate each day, but if you try to end the day with some gratitude for all you have experienced, felt, and lived, you'll find you have a more positive outlook. To end your day with some gratitude, try a sunset mindfulness practice:

- As you watch the colors change across the sky and the sun slide down toward the earth, let it bring to mind the inevitability of change. Each day you face enormous change. Change is an inevitable part of life, and sunsets help you remember that.
- Remind yourself to feel grateful for the day that you were given and to foster appreciation for the opportunities you had in this day.
- Keep your attention on the sunset and gently bring your thoughts back to it if you catch them wandering off.
- Notice how time passes as you focus on the sun's gradual journey out of sight. Note whether it feels fast, slow, or somewhere in between. Think about what that means—if it feels slow, are you anxious to get off to your next appointment? If so, gently push that anxiety out of your mind. If it feels fast, are you hanging on too tightly to this one moment in time? If so, gently remind yourself that the sun rises and sets each day.
- As the sun sinks low and eventually disappears, embrace the coming darkness as the inevitable progression after light, as well as a precursor to the inevitable return of light.

Allow yourself to relax into your more natural state after the sun has set, then appreciate how wonderful it is to be able to enjoy a sunset.

DO THE OPPOSITE

People high in resilience generally don't waste much time dwelling on their sorrows. When they get knocked down, they might take some time to gather their thoughts and engage in some vital self-care, but before long they're getting back on their feet and deciding on their next move.

When you are feeling burned out and low in resilience, you do the opposite—you stay where you are or even take a few steps back. Although this is an understandable urge, it usually isn't effective.

One way to build up your resilience is to do the opposite—meaning do the *opposite of what you would usually do*!

If you usually go home and wrap yourself in a blanket when you face disappointment, try going out for dinner or drinks with friends instead.

If your first instinct is to quit something when you run into a particularly difficult situation, try sticking it out and doubling down on your commitment.

If your go-to coping method is indulging in junk food, look up some new healthy recipes and get cooking!

Your feelings have a strong influence over your actions, but they don't have to decide your actions for you. By doing the opposite of whatever you feel like doing when faced with failure or disappointment, you are training yourself to make better decisions whether you feel like it or not and helping to break out of the burnout cycle.

FORGIVE YOURSELF

The simplest way to have a sunnier outlook is to just cut yourself some slack. As humans, we are often our own worst critics—and when we mess up or do something we disapprove of, it's hard to let it go and forgive ourselves for the harm we've caused. However, feeling negative and guilty will cause a dramatic and instantaneous drop in your mood and self-confidence! So use the power of forgiveness in two ways to boost yourself up and spark happiness:

1. If you're feeling guilty and beating yourself up at the time of the incident, it's okay to feel bad—acknowledge it. However, move on from there. Accept and forgive yourself. Use your mistake as a learning step so you can avoid making the same mistake in the future, and let it pass. Look ahead and feel energized about being better in the future.

2. If you're in need of a quick emotional lift, it's time to let go of something you did in the past but never came to terms with. Forgive yourself for an argument, a missed work deadline, or even something as simple as forgetting to hold the door open for someone.

By freeing yourself of the weight on your shoulders, you'll feel lighter on your feet with more energy and glee.

WRITE A POEM ABOUT JOY

Some people may read the title of this exercise and think, "No way!" But don't worry if you're not a poet by nature. You don't need to write good poetry for this exercise to work; you only need to write authentically and from the heart. The point of this exercise is to get you thinking about joy, because when you focus on joy, your mind is encouraged to be happy; therefore, it helps combat the sadness and negativity that can come from feeling burned out.

First, start by taking a few minutes to reflect on the experience of joy. Think about what it feels like when you are joyful. Ask yourself questions like:

- Does your heart beat faster or slower?
- Does your mind slow down or speed up?
- How does your body feel when you are full of joy?
- What emotions often go hand in hand with joy?

Once you have a good idea of what it feels like for you to experience joy, start putting together your piece. Use your answers to the previous questions to come up with a work that you could use to describe your experience of joy for someone else. You can think of it as a poem, a song, or simply a string of words and phrases that accurately capture your personal experience of joy.

Now you'll have a happy reminder you can read whenever you want to recapture that feeling of joy!

BALANCE PRIDE AND HUMILITY

The gentle virtue of humility can help you with the stress of workplace burnout. In the ancient Hindu scripture the Bhagavad Gita, Lord Krishna advises his disciple Arjuna to work to the best of his ability and to give up any attachment to the results, remaining "calm in both success and failure." Being able to remain calm at your job no matter what the circumstance will allow that peace to infiltrate your being and reduce your stress. No matter what your job, or where you work, taking the time to balance the pride of your accomplishments with humility will lead you to a happier, more positive place.

1. Take time to sit quietly and reflect on how to balance pride with humility in your line of work. Vow to receive praise when you deserve it with graceful thanks. Don't say, "It was nothing," because that is dishonest. Eschew fishing for compliments.

2. Enter a quiet concentration on why holding to a calm serenity is paramount. Think only on this point, do not allow other thoughts to enter your mind.

3. Ask your higher power or the universe for help on the job as you work to remain balanced even in the flurry of activity—regardless of how hectic and crazy work becomes.

CREATE A POSITIVE JOURNAL

Journaling is a great practice for many reasons: It can help you make sense of jumbled thoughts, it can help you work through your emotions, and it can facilitate self-reflection. Including both positive and negative experiences in your entries is important for authenticity.

However, if you're feeling down and looking to boost your optimism, you might want to try keeping a positive diary. As the name implies, this is a diary in which you focus only on the positive experiences you have.

Each night, just before bed, take out your positive journal and go over your day, scanning for the good things that happened. These can include good things that happened to you, good things that you witnessed happening to others, or even good things you did for yourself or for others. Basically, if it happened in the last day and it can be described as positive, write it down!

If you had a particularly excellent meal, write it down. If you saw a romantic public proposal, write it down. If you offered your assistance to a friend in need, write it down. You get the picture—if it was good, write it down!

Each day, you will create a list of new reasons to smile and be optimistic. This is an excellent way to make sure you end your day on a positive note.

PRACTICE 2-MINUTE KINDNESS

Doing something kind for another person is an easy way to fight the stress of burnout and provide yourself with a boost of good feelings. Although humans have the potential to be quite nasty to one another, the urge to act kindly is also a strong one, and it can have lasting effects.

At some point in your day, take a 2-minute break to do something kind for someone else. You can do anything you'd like, as long as it is kind and it takes no more than 2 minutes. If you're not sure where to start with your 2-minute kindness, consider trying one of these example acts:

1. Take 2 minutes to write a short email or text message praising a coworker or complimenting a friend.

2. Strike up a quick, casual conversation with the shy new person at school or in the office while you're on your way to your next class or meeting.

3. If you see someone drop his or her groceries or mail, stop and take a minute or two to help him or her pick everything up and put everything back in order.

If none of these examples sound relevant to you, choose whatever act of kindness comes naturally to you. Using just 2 minutes of your day to do something kind for others will have a much larger impact on your happiness than you can imagine.

SAY A PRAYER

Prayer can have some incredible positive effects on your life. Whether prayers are "answered" or not, the simple act of praying itself usually leaves you calmer and happier than you were before. And it's not only prayer—meditating, practicing mindfulness, or any form of communication with a higher power can all lead to the same outcomes.

If burnout is making you defeated and low, try saying a quick prayer to give you hope for the future and motivation to keep going. All you need to do is come up with something to say to the universe, God, or your higher power of choice. If you consider yourself religious or spiritual, you likely won't have a problem coming up with a prayer!

If you do have trouble, try sending this quick thought out into the universe:

"I am alive, I am whole, I am present, and I am grateful for these gifts."

It's that simple! Give it a shot—saying even a brief prayer (and really meaning what you say) is a quick ticket to a more blissful mood.

LIST YOUR WISHES

If you want to combat burnout and cultivate a steady and present sense of positivity in your life, you need to make sure that you have goals to work toward and things to look forward to. To do this try listing your wishes.

You can do this in your head, but it's best to record them somewhere, like your journal, a phone app, or even a random scrap of paper.

Create your list by writing down the things that really drive you, excite you, or get you fired up. For example:

- What do you want to happen in your future?
- What would your dream job be?
- Do you hope to win a Nobel Prize?
- Where have you always wanted to travel?
- Have you always dreamed of starting your own business?
- Do you want to lose some weight?
- What would your dream house look like?
- What is your perfect mate like?

Whatever you desire most, write it down. It doesn't matter if it seems far-fetched or if you feel like it will take way too much effort to get there—your goals and wishes should stretch and challenge you.

VOLUNTEER

When you are feeling down and burned out by your life, sometimes all it takes to feel better is to focus on helping others. Helping others has been shown to reduce stress, combat depression, keep you mentally stimulated, and give you a greater sense of purpose.

Find an organization that you like or that really speaks to you and your values. If you're an animal lover, the local shelter might be a good option. If you're passionate about at-risk youth, find a Big Brothers Big Sisters of America chapter or similar mentoring program. If you have family members or friends who have struggled with homelessness, find a local soup kitchen.

Whichever organization you pick, look online or call to find volunteer opportunities. If you can sign up online, do it. If you can commit to volunteering at a certain time and place over the phone, do it.

Simply deciding to spend some of your time giving to others and contributing to a good cause can make you feel better— just make sure you follow through on it and get an even bigger payoff of happiness!

BALANCE WHAT YOU LIKE TO DO WITH WHAT YOU HAVE TO DO

This exercise is based on the idea that balance is where happiness can be found. We all have to do things we don't want to in our lives, but that doesn't mean you simply throw up your hands and give in. There are some things you may be able to craft, change, or alter to make those things more palatable to you.

Get out your journal or a piece of notebook paper and draw two columns. Label Column 1 "Things I Like to Do," and label Column 2 "Things I Have to Do."

Under Column 1, list things that are not essential for your day-to-day survival but that help you live a happy and fulfilling life. For example, you would not write "eating" here, but you might write "indulging in an occasional happy hour snack."

Under Column 2, list the things that *are* essential for you to function as an independent adult. You might write things like "going to work" or "getting my oil changed" in this column.

Compare the two columns and ask yourself these questions:

- Which things in Column 1 are especially good for my well-being?
- Which things in Column 2 do I particularly dislike doing?

Try to come up with ways to combine these two sets of activities into your daily routine, especially those that you don't generally enjoy. For instance, if listening to music is in Column 1 and vacuuming is in Column 2, try vacuuming with your headphones on next time.

FAKE IT 'TIL YOU CAN MAKE IT

You probably heard this phrase from a parent or teacher at some point as encouragement for doing something you were anxious or insecure about doing. He or she probably told you that most people don't know what they're doing, but they figure it out as they go.

Well, as you've surely noticed in your own life, that person was right! Many of us try new things with no prior knowledge or experience and just figure it out while doing it. Lots of people take new positions they don't feel ready for, but apply themselves to learning on the job.

"Fake it 'til you make it" is a surprisingly common learning technique, and it is one that works for learning optimism as well. Instead of trying to force yourself to think positively, try simply *acting* like you're thinking positively. Even if your burnout symptoms have you predicting doom and gloom on the inside, do what an optimist would do. Think about what a person expecting a positive outcome would do and commit to taking the same actions. After all, your thoughts don't need to match your actions. You don't have to be expecting the worst to prepare for it, and you don't need to feel particularly cheery to plan for the best.

Eventually, that positive outer attitude will begin to seep in, creating a positive inner attitude as well.

MAKE A MINI VISION BOARD

When feeling burned out has you pessimistic about your future, try making a vision board to motivate you. Vision boards are excellent tools to help you solidify your dreams and make your goals seem closer and more achievable than ever. This feeling of being competent enough to accomplish your goals carries a lot of other good feelings with it.

To make a mini vision board, follow these steps:

1. Grab a piece of card stock, cardboard, or another sturdy background for your mini vision board. It shouldn't be more than about a foot on each side.

2. Get some images that represent your most desired goal. You can draw these, download them from the Internet, cut them out of magazines, or grab some old photos.

3. Arrange the images to correspond to your goals. For example, if your goal is to backpack across Europe, you might have some images of backpacks, popular destinations in Europe, travelers, or beautiful scenery.

4. Optional: Add some color, glitter, ribbon, or any other type of embellishment to make your vision board visually appealing.

Hang it where you will see it often, and let it bring you inspiration every time it catches your eye!

FIGHT MIND CHATTER

The increased mind chatter that comes in our fast-paced world of multitasking, stress, and burnout can make you feel like there is never any calm or mental clarity in your life. When mind chatter disturbs your thoughts, you miss the full content of each moment and lose your chance of finding peace. Fortunately, this meditation can help you calm those mental mind waves of distraction.

1. Sit and meditate in the stillness of a quiet space where you won't be disturbed. Sit in any pose that feels comfortable. Don't strain to hold a pose, since that will just add more mind chatter.

2. Pull your attention inward and close your eyes.

3. Allow free association of your thoughts. Let them go until they slowly decrease in their arising and falling away.

4. Mentally affirm: "I am the watcher of the mind. I feel calm and focused. I will ride the waves of my thoughts until they disappear into the ocean of peace."

5. Reflect on the change that is always possible through a shift in priorities, attitude, and action.

CRAFT YOUR PERFECT DAY

We are busy people—busier than ever in our modern world—and we rarely have time to take an entire day to simply indulge and enjoy ourselves. This is one reason so many of us feel burned out and overwhelmed with life! Luckily, you don't need an entire day to get a little boost of happiness! All you need is a few minutes to plan out your perfect day.

Sit down and think about how you would spend your time if you had an entire day of freedom: no work, no school, and no responsibilities.

Outline exactly how you would spend this day. For example, you might write:

- Sleep in until 9:00 a.m.
- Eat at my favorite brunch spot.
- See a movie with a good friend.
- Curl up in the window seat and read for an hour.
- Take a long, relaxing walk with my spouse or significant other.
- Make dinner together and share a bottle of wine.
- Host a game night with friends.
- Head to bed around 11:00 p.m.

You'll find that just planning your perfect day can give you a bit of the joy that actually living it would!

DOCUMENT LESSONS LEARNED

We have all suffered from setbacks, but if you're reading this, you're still here! That means that you have recovered from past bumps in the road. Figuring out the tools you used to do this will help you improve your ability to rebound in the future.

To figure out how you survived and thrived through your troubles in the past, you need to conduct an investigation into your lessons learned. In a business context, this term usually refers to a post–project-completion review or reflection on what worked well, what didn't, and what you learned about how to make future projects run smoother.

You will consider the same aspects except in the context of your personal development. Follow these steps to conduct a lessons-learned reflection:

1. Think about one of the most difficult setbacks or failures you have experienced. Describe it in detail.

2. Reflect on how you made it through. Ask yourself:
- What helped me get through?
- What did I do that made the situation more difficult?
- If I faced a similar situation, what would I do the same and what would I do differently?

3. Wrap it all up in a set of bullet points on how you can successfully make it through any difficult situation.

Refer to these bullet points to identify your best strategies for bouncing back from burnout.

WATCH THAT NEGATIVE LANGUAGE

When you are burned out, you may feel more depressed and cynical, but using negative language on yourself is not the answer. This language is demoralizing, and it can also hold you back from being your best self.

This exercise will help you to be more aware of the negative language you use with yourself and come up with alternative language to replace those unhelpful thoughts.

Follow these three simple steps:

1. Start checking in regularly with your thoughts. Train yourself to pause your train of thought at least a few times a day and scan for any negative language you are using with yourself.

2. Identify the negative language. You will quickly learn which words and phrases you use the most often. For example, you may frequently catch yourself saying, "There's no way that I can..." or "I always screw up when...."

3. Replace the negative language. Instead of thinking to yourself, "There's no way that I can...," try "It might work out...." And instead of thinking, "I always screw up when...," replace the thought with "I usually succeed when...."

Replacing the negative language with more helpful, optimistic language will help you develop a new tendency to look on the bright side.

FOCUS ON A FEW GOOD MEMORIES

When the hectic pace of your days seems to be taking a toll on you, taking a few minutes to reflect on some happy memories is a healthy practice and a good way to make you feel more joyful. No matter who you are or where you've been, you have some fond memories to look back on.

1. Think about your happiest memories and come up with a list of four or five.

2. Think about each of these memories in turn, focusing on what it felt like to be that happy. Try to recreate that feeling inside you.

3. For each memory, write down one word that best captures how you felt in the moment. For example, if one of your happiest memories was graduating from college, you might write "Proud."

4. Once you have selected a word for each memory, look at the list and read it out loud to yourself. Think about how wonderful it is that you are able to feel such wonderful feelings, remind yourself that you deserve to feel these feelings, and be grateful that you have experienced them.

VISUALIZE A POSITIVE FUTURE

This exercise works by helping you visualize one of your many positive potential futures. Allowing yourself to believe in a positive future is a fundamental piece of being optimistic, and visualizing a positive and realistic version of yourself can help you get there.

Take some time to think about the goals you have set for your life that are most important to you. Consider how likely it is for you to reach all of these goals within one lifetime. Which goals are compatible with one another? Are any goals incompatible? What goals would you be willing to sacrifice if it meant you could meet other goals?

From your answers to these questions, build a mental image of what this future will look like and how it will feel to have met the goals you identified as most important. Gather as much detail as you can: Who are you with? What are you doing? Where are you are living? How are you feeling? Think about whether you would feel regret over not meeting each of the goals you originally set for yourself, or whether you would feel satisfied and fulfilled focusing on the goals you *have* met.

This exercise can be especially helpful when you are feeling overwhelmed, since it reminds you that it's okay to let some things go—you can still be a happy and fulfilled person, even if you don't meet each and every goal you set for yourself!

HOLD ON TO YOUR DREAMS

The late Steve Jobs said that time is limited and we should not waste it living someone else's life, nor should we be trapped by the dogma of other people's thinking—our own thoughts drowned out by theirs. Your dream is yours. Don't give others the power to push you into abandoning it. That dream is your treasure. If you hope to make it come true, then own that. Get to work manifesting that dream through the power of positive thinking and feeling, affirmations, visualizations, and gratitude for the blessings you already have in your life.

1. Write out your dream on a piece of self-stick paper. Place this note in a location where you will see it often, to keep reminding you of what it is calling you to do.

2. Sit quietly and slow your thoughts.

3. Declare your intention. Focus on your dream, and know that it is possible and it is yours to have. Already, your intention is stirring the field of infinite potential and drawing itself into manifestation.

4. Use affirmation or visualization (or both) to reinforce your hope of having that dream come into your world.

5. Abolish all doubt and feel confidently expectant.

6. Thank your higher power or the universe that makes all things possible.

Having a dream or something to strive for will give you hope when the stress and depression of burnout try to overwhelm you.

PRACTICE JOYFUL LIVING

The secret to battling the stress and depression of burnout is practicing joyful living as a way of life. Joyful living is going through life with your eyes wide open to find the good, the positive, the awe-inspiring, and the uplifting all around you.

To open yourself up to experiencing happiness on a daily basis, give joyful living a test run. Here's what to do:

- Set aside a few minutes to practice, wherever you are and whatever is going on around you.
- Set an intention to find joy in anything that comes your way, no matter what it is.
- For those few minutes, practice finding joy in whatever happens.

If the barista at a coffeehouse mispronounces your name, find joy in laughing about it. If you learn that your favorite lunch spot is closed for renovations, find joy in the opportunity to try a new cuisine.

Joy can be found just about everywhere, if you only open your eyes and look for it.

Chapter 5

REFUEL
YOUR
≥RELATIONSHIPS≤

This chapter is all about relationships: how to establish healthy ones, how to maintain current ones, and how good relationships can buffer you from the effects of burnout. Having a strong social support system around you is vital to your mental health and well-being. When burnout has you feeling disconnected and detached, working on your relationships with others is the only way to recover. You will need solid, reliable relationships with friends and family to lean on, draw strength from, and get advice and encouragement from. If you're not sure that your relationships are strong enough to provide you with the support you need, you might want to spend some time building them up.

These exercises will provide you with fifty different ways to do just that. You will find practical tips and suggestions to connect with those around you, strengthen your relationships with friends and family, and deepen your relationship with your partner. Some of them will only take a few minutes, while others might require a few hours—just flip through the pages to find one that suits your current needs and any time constraints you have.

GIVE OR RECEIVE A MASSAGE

Nothing promotes the sense of healing and nurturing as much as the human touch. We all need it, and we all suffer when we don't experience it. Why? Because when your skin is touched, your brain releases oxytocin, a hormone that helps you relax and form closer emotional connections with others. When you're feeling burned out, a boost of oxytocin might be just what you need to feel restored. The good news is that we benefit when we receive touch from others *and* when we give our touch to others.

To get a healthy dose of good, old-fashioned human touch, offer a massage to a loved one. If you don't think you have the skills to give a top-notch massage, search online for videos or articles that can teach you, or consider going to get a couples massage—they're not just for couples! You can get a massage as any sort of duo: mother and daughter, sisters, friends, lovers...any combination of you and a loved one is acceptable. Many spas offer a variety of massages, including the typical Japanese, Swedish, Ayurvedic, and myriad other types. Some even include aromatherapy and a relaxing dip in the pool, or you can opt to stay in the sauna before the massage, which can increase your relaxation as well as give you a chance to catch up or have a heart-to-heart with your loved one. Harness the power of touch to revitalize your relationships and your own well-being.

PRACTICE YOGA WITH SOMEONE YOU CARE ABOUT

Yoga is not only an excellent way to unwind, relax, and strengthen your body; it's also a great way to connect with yourself and with others. It offers you an opportunity to expand and deepen your bond with those you invite into your practice, all while recharging your internal batteries and building a greater sense of well-being.

To take advantage of all that yoga has to offer, ask a friend or family member to accompany you to your yoga class. If you don't attend any yoga classes, find one of the many videos online that can guide you through a yoga practice. All you need is two yoga mats and space to stretch, then you'll have all the tools required to refuel and renew with a loved one.

For added challenge and connection potential, look up yoga moves meant for two. Rely on one another as you stretch, twist, and reach. Partner poses add the element of physical touch, which will help you connect more with your yoga partner and experience even more relaxation thanks to the oxytocin your brain is releasing in response to touch. Trust each other as you practice balance moves and encourage each other through strength-building moves. You'll find that your body isn't the only thing getting stronger; you are also enhancing your mental well-being, your relationship with your loved one, and your ability to bounce back and recover from burnout.

GAIN NEW PERSPECTIVES BY ENGAGING IN HEALTHY DEBATES

When good friends get together for drinks or a meal, it can be fun to talk about all the subjects that you are told not to bring up in polite company—things like sex, politics, and religion. A healthy debate can clarify your understanding of a subject, stimulate your mind, and trigger new ideas. Let the intensity of the discussion reignite your passion, vision, and purpose when you're feeling burned out.

To give this a try, recruit a couple of friends, but make sure they're on board with your mission to discuss topics that can be "taboo," or you might find yourself engaging in decidedly unfriendly conversation! Let your friends know you plan on being open-minded, objective, and welcoming to new ideas and ask they do the same. Seek to open your friends' minds, but don't stop there. Let them open your mind as well. Ask questions. Seek honest answers. Engage in vigorous debate. Listen attentively. Respond thoughtfully.

If at any point the discussion gets overly heated or emotional, back down from the debate and segue into less controversial topics. Reestablish your friendly relationships and affirm your genuine care and affection for one another before attempting to dive back into more sensitive subjects. Good friendships can not only withstand heated debate, they can also be strengthened by them.

ORCHESTRATE A SPA DAY WITH YOUR FRIENDS

What's better for preventing burnout than having a relaxing day getting pampered? Having a relaxing day getting pampered *with your friends*!

Taking care of your body is a great way to practice self-care. When you feel stressed, you might not realize the impact it is having on your body, but it's something you really should pay attention to. Stress can cause you to feel tired, achy, tense, fatigued, and sore—often without realizing why. You can also find yourself acting in ways that are detrimental to your relationships with loved ones, even pulling away and isolating yourself from them. It can be tempting to let yourself slide down this slippery slope, or to rely on grabbing drinks to bolster your relationships.

To give stress and burnout the one–two punch, organize something that will benefit both your body and your relationships: a spa day! You can invite your close friends to meet you at the spa instead of happy hour and sip cucumber water in place of cocktails.

Alternatively, you could set up a spa day that doesn't require leaving the house! Arrange for a massage therapist, a manicurist, and a hair and makeup expert to pamper you and your friends in the comfort of your own home. Let yourself sink into the relaxation and enjoy extra bonding time with your loved ones.

ACT AS A CRISIS COACH

Sometimes, the best medicine to heal yourself is to focus on helping others. Reaching out and lifting up a friend can help you lift yourself up as well. Think about someone in your life who is going through a rough time. Maybe he or she is getting divorced, dealing with the death of a parent, or struggling to find work after being laid off. Whatever he or she is dealing with, make it a point to reach out—and not just once.

Commit to being a consistent presence in your friend's life. Plan a time every morning or evening to chat on the phone with your friend or meet up for coffee or lunch (as your schedule allows). Don't set any expectations or make any demands of your friend; simply make yourself available for whatever he or she needs at the moment. Encourage your friend to share his or her burden with you, and let him or her know you're there to help, to talk, to listen, or even to just sit in companionable silence.

Being someone else's shoulder not only helps him or her; it also gives you a sense of purpose and helps you build your relationship into an even stronger bond. Reach out to someone in need, and you'll be surprised at how much it affects you!

GO OUT OF YOUR WAY FOR A FRIEND

This is a great idea for two reasons—it gives you something productive (and hopefully fun) to do, and it strengthens your relationship with your loved one! The dual benefits make this exercise doubly impactful on your stress level and well-being.

If you know a friend who needs help with something, great! You know where to start. Is a friend starting a new business? Offer to lend a hand. Does your friend need some help with a big project in their house or yard? Head on over with your hard hat or gardening gloves. Do you know someone who just needs a ride from the airport that's over an hour away? Tell them not to worry, you'll be there at the curb!

If you don't know of a friend who could use a friendly hand, your task is a little more involved, but it's even more important. Start by reaching out to some friends that you haven't spoken with in a while. It's easy to fall out of touch and feel disconnected, even in our constantly connected world, but reforging that connection could take just one quick call or text. Find out who in your circle needs help, and either offer to help or just jump right in and do it!

It will make you feel good, boost their mood, and give you an even better buffer against burnout.

LET A LOVED ONE GO OUT OF HIS OR HER WAY FOR YOU

It's great to go out of your way for someone you love. You get to do something nice and show just how much you love him or her, and it makes you feel good! However, if you're a giver by nature, you might not allow your loved ones to do the same for you.

Taking everything on by yourself is often one of the factors that leads to burnout; when you don't feel like it's okay to ask for help, you can quickly find yourself drowning. It's more than okay to ask for help—it's a necessity! You can't do everything on your own, nor should you.

This may be tougher than the previous exercise, but force yourself to do the opposite of going out of your way for a friend and let someone do the same for you. If loved ones ask you how they can help, be honest! Give them ways to relieve your burden and allow them to actually do it. You'll find it's quite nice being taken care of once in a while, and it doesn't make you any less of a strong, capable person.

PLAY MATCHMAKER WITH YOUR (SINGLE) LOVED ONES

Love is an excellent preventative tool *and* cure for stress and burnout—even when you're not the direct recipient or giver! Just being around two people in love can be a salve for a sad heart and a boost of hope for those feeling downtrodden. But how do you find such a positive and heartwarming dose of lovey goodness? By orchestrating it!

Acting as a matchmaker can be a blast. You get to introduce two people whose company you already enjoy and potentially plant the seeds for a relationship that could make them both even more joyful and full of life. Plus, if it works out, you get to be featured in their "how we met" story as the force that brought the two of them together!

If you're not sure about just setting up two friends on a blind date, consider throwing a party and inviting them both. When they have both arrived, make sure to introduce them to each other warmly and include fun and interesting facts about them both. Who knows...they may spend the rest of their married lives thanking you!

WRITE A GRATITUDE LETTER

Gratitude may be the single best tool you have in your toolbox to ward off burnout and enhance your own well-being. Making it a habit to practice gratitude can make you more positive and optimistic, help you bounce back from hardships, and even make you physically healthier!

To practice gratitude and give your relationship a boost at the same time, try writing a gratitude letter to someone you love. It doesn't have to be full of poetry or flowery words, and you don't need to spend money on a gift, flowers, or a fancy card—all you really need to show someone you appreciate him or her is to be honest and tell that person how you feel about him or her.

Think of someone who has had a positive impact on your life. It could be anyone, but if you're having trouble thinking of someone, consider a parent, sibling, close friend, or mentor. Sit down and take a few minutes to think about all the ways this person has improved your life. Once you have a list of the biggest and most meaningful things this person has done for you, pour your heart out! Write a letter detailing how he or she has enhanced your life and how much you care about him or her. You can either send the letter via email or snail mail, or—the more impactful option—you can hand-deliver it and even read it out loud!

ACCEPT YOUR FRIEND AS HE/SHE IS

It's easy to say you love the people in your life exactly as they are, but it's harder to do and harder to show. However, accepting our loved ones as they are and refraining from trying to control or change them is one of the best moves you can make in terms of building a healthy social support system—both for you and for them!

To work on accepting your loved ones as they are, try this thought exercise. Remind yourself that there is only one person on the planet who you have control over: yourself! As much as you may like to think you have strong influence on those around you, it's simply not possible—or ethical—to control someone else. Recognize that you are your own unique person with your own unique talents, gifts, weaknesses, likes, dislikes, and interests. Just as you would hate for a friend or family member to try to bend you to his or her will, realize that those you love also value their freedom and individuality.

Commit to accepting your friends for the wonderful and one-of-a-kind people they are, and brainstorm some ways to show it.

DELIVER SOME HOMEMADE GOODIES

What's a better way to show you care than sending someone some store-bought treats? Delivering *homemade* goodies straight to their door!

Cooking or baking for your loved ones is a great way to show them you care, and it gives you a chance to practice some of your own skills and enjoy your own tasty treat at the same time. There's something so much more personal and meaningful when you use your own hands to prepare a delicious bite for someone. Plus, it gives you an extra boost of the feel-goods when you put some extra effort into doing something nice for others!

If you have a signature dish or favorite recipe, whip up a batch of whatever it is and hand-deliver it to a loved one. This can be most effective for those who are struggling (e.g., dealing with a death in the family), but just about anyone is sure to enjoy the fruits of your labor. Remind your friend or family member that the goodies were made with love and that there is no expectation of a reward or reciprocation, then revel in your loved one's happy smile. Build your relationships when times are good, and you will thank yourself during your more difficult days.

TAKE DANCE LESSONS WITH A BUDDY

When the sadness and depression of burnout make you want to curl up in a ball on your couch, try dancing to lift you out of that funk. Dancing is good for the body and the soul! It's also a fabulous way to have some fun, boost your mood, and even enhance your relationships with your dance partners. Learning to dance, especially when it's a particularly physical or complex dance, can be a real challenge. Embrace the challenge—and your loved one—with open arms.

There are tons of different types of dance, so make sure to take a look at the full menu of styles, and find something that appeals to you and your loved one. Whatever your preference, there is sure to be a dance class or tutor in your area to help you pick up a new skill. If you're hoping to pick it up quickly, one-on-one lessons might be best. On the other hand, if you're looking to learn on a budget, group classes might be right for you.

Discuss what you want out of these lessons with your loved one to make sure you're on the same page: Are you just looking to have fun, or do you want to wow a crowd with a choreographed dance? Decide on your goals and commit to giving it your all and growing together!

LET A LOVED ONE TEACH YOU SOMETHING NEW

When you gain new skills or improve an existing skill set in any area of your life, you are teaching yourself how to do one of the most important things in life: how to learn and grow.

Boost your resilience and defend against burnout by asking a friend to teach you one of his or her most valued skills. Do you have a friend who is a great guitar player? Perhaps you've always admired a friend's garden or respected a loved one's budgeting skills. Whatever skill you admire, reach out to your friend and ask if he or she wouldn't mind giving you a crash course.

Not only will learning a new skill keep you happy and mentally healthy, you will likely make your friend's day by complimenting him or her and giving that person a chance to engage in something that he or she excels at. You can offer to pay your friend or return the favor with teaching him or her a bit about your own unique skills, but people are generally pretty happy to share their tips and tricks with those they love.

When you get started learning the skill, make sure to pay attention to the lessons and show your loved one your respect and admiration.

PAY IT FORWARD

As you probably already know, "paying it forward" refers to the act of passing on the good feelings you get when someone does something nice for you. It's great to be on the receiving end of a kind act, but it can feel even better to be the giver!

Think about something a friend or loved one did for you recently that made your day. It doesn't necessarily need to be something huge; even something as small as having someone pick up and deliver your coffee order or giving you a compliment can be paid forward. Once you have the generous act in mind, take a few moments to think about how great it was to have someone do something nice for you.

Next, decide on how you'd like to continue the chain of good deeds. Find a target for your niceness and consider what they need or what you could do to enhance their day. You might choose something like sending them an anonymous gift card to their favorite restaurant or taking on one of their least favorite chores or tasks. Whatever you do, your loved one is sure to see your effort and appreciate it. This will boost your relationship with that person and help mold you into a kinder and more considerate person, one "payback" at a time.

ALLOW YOUR FRIENDS TO PAY IT BACK

After paying it forward to someone else, try another great relationship-boosting exercise by allowing your friends to "pay it back." Sometimes we get caught up in paying our own debts or ensuring that we don't owe anyone anything, but we tend to forget that other people feel like that as well. It's great to pay someone back and feel a load lifted off of your shoulders, but it also feels great to help unburden someone else.

If you recently did favors for friends or helped them out with something important and they want the chance to repay you, let them! Instead of brushing it aside or saying, "No worries! You can just get me back later," accept their offer and thank them graciously.

Showing your friends that you acknowledge and appreciate that they remembered to pay you back for whatever favor you did for them will generate those warm, fuzzy feelings that can take your relationship from good to great. It will also open the door to more honest and open communication, something that can help when you need candid advice or a compassionate heart-to-heart in tough times.

FOCUS ON YOUR FRIEND

It's easy to focus on yourself, especially in the era of self-care. Self-care is vital to being happy and healthy, but you should be careful not to get too caught up in your own wants and needs. Once you have met the minimum for effective self-care, boost your relationship with a friend by focusing on him or her.

Instead of thinking about what you'd like to do or what would make you feel better about yourself or your life in this moment, take a few minutes to put yourself in your friend's shoes: What does he or she need to feel good right now? What are his or her favorite activities? What cheers your friend up when he or she is feeling overwhelmed or under the weather?

If you're not sure, ask! It will spark a meaningful conversation in which you both learn more about the other person and strengthen the foundation of your friendship. Focusing on someone else's wants and needs can even give you a feeling of release, as if you have given yourself permission to be okay as you are and take comfort and joy in providing care for a friend.

BRING A LOVED ONE HIS OR HER FAVORITE BEVERAGE

Have you ever had a rough day that was immediately brightened when someone made a Starbucks run or showed up with your favorite flavor of boba tea? Remember how great that felt to be on the receiving end of an act of kindness, even one as small as picking up a coffee for you? If you're feeling down or despondent, try being on the giving end of this exercise.

Doing something nice for your loved one will not only make his or her day; it will remind you of the time(s) when someone did the same for you, making you feel loved and appreciated all over again. Make sure to check in with your loved one if you're not sure what his or her favorite beverage is, so you don't show up with something that person would never order!

When you drop it off, do so with a smile and an assurance that you have no expectations of your friend repaying the favor right away—or at all. This is an important piece of the exercise, because it will establish that your relationship is not transactional, but based on mutual love and affection. If you're feeling stressed or burned out, this can give you the boost in mood you need to feel rejuvenated!

SWAP SKILLS WITH A FRIEND

We all have our own set of skills and talents. Each set is a unique set—one that is not quite like anyone else's. This makes life more interesting and underscores the need for good relationships, since we all rely on others to fill in our skill gaps. For example, most people pay someone to do their taxes since that is not an area that they have knowledge or skill in.

To combat burnout and connect with your loved ones, you can try asking someone to help you with something that you don't have the knowledge or skill to tackle. You might feel like you're being a burden by asking someone to use their skill set for you, but that's where the swap comes in. If you suggest swapping skills instead of asking for a one-way exchange, you won't feel like you're being needy or asking for too much.

Besides, people generally like to be able to use their skills for those they love! It's nice to feel useful, valued, and respected, and it's great to know that you helped someone with a task that would be really difficult or challenging for them on their own. Ask around and see which friend or family member has a skill that you could put to use, and see if there's anything you can offer them in return.

HELP SOMEONE WHO'S GRIEVING

We can often get caught up in our own woes when we're going through a tough time. If you're stressed, you're probably thinking about what's going on in your own life—particularly what's going wrong—rather than the challenges someone else is facing. This is a natural reaction, but not one that's particularly useful in helping you feel better.

Instead of getting caught up in your own troubles, think about what other people in your life are going through. If one of your friends or family members is grieving, this presents you with a good opportunity to put your challenges into perspective. Not only will this help you feel a little better about what's going on in your life, it also provides you with a chance to do something good.

Reach out to this loved one and see what you can do to help and support them as they work through the grieving process. They may need someone to simply sit with them in silence, or might need some premade meals at the ready in the fridge. Help your loved one however you can, and you will both strengthen your relationship and enhance your ability to practice compassion—an ability that can come in handy when you need to show yourself a little compassion.

COMMIT TO A GOAL WITH A LOVED ONE

If you've ever tried to lose a significant amount of weight, train for a marathon, or some other challenging long-term goal, you know how tough it can be to stick to it. But if you've succeeded in a goal like this, you also know the sense of satisfaction you can receive from your success!

Many people accomplish large goals by doing it alone, but you can enhance your chances of success and get more fulfillment out of it if you enlist a buddy to help keep you accountable and celebrate with you. It can also be incredibly helpful for your loved one to help him or her work toward a difficult goal. Perhaps he or she is not up to taking on this task alone, or he or she lacks the motivation to get started— until you join him or her on the journey!

Find out whether you and any of your loved ones have a similar goal in mind, and talk to him or her about committing to it together. Sell your loved one on it by describing how you can motivate and support one another when the going gets tough, and tell him or her to imagine how great it will feel to accomplish something together.

Once you both are on board, decide together on exactly what your goal is, how to define it, and put together a game plan for how you will work toward it.

PLAY A BOARD GAME WITH A BUDDY

Board games are a great way to relax, unwind, and have some fun! When you're feeling stressed and burned out, a little fun and relaxation is likely exactly what you need. If you're worried about taking time away from important tasks to do something that feels so frivolous, remind yourself that it's vital to take breaks once in a while. A happy, relaxed you is much more efficient than a stressed, tense you!

Grab a buddy who is on board and find a game to play together. There are classic board games—like Monopoly, The Game of Life, and Risk—that are classic for a reason! However, you might like to branch out into new territory and learn something new together. There are hundreds—if not thousands—of board games out there that you can play. If you're not sure where to start, The Settlers of Catan is known as the "gateway board game" and for good reason— it's pretty easy to learn and fun to play!

Give yourself permission to unwind and enjoy the game, and try to keep work and other stressors out of your mind, just for a couple of hours. To up the enjoyment, get some yummy snacks to complement your game.

ASK SOMEONE TO HELP YOU WITH SPRING CLEANING

What's a chore we all have on our list that we generally are not thrilled about doing? *Spring cleaning!* Whether you have a huge house or a tiny apartment, you'll need to set aside some time for deep cleaning at some point (even if it's not in the spring), and it's probably not something you are looking forward to.

To help you tackle such a big chore, consider enlisting the help of a friend or family member. Not only will you cut the cleaning time in half, you'll have someone there to distract you from the drudgery and perhaps even take on the tasks you like the least. For example, if your friend hates cleaning toilets and you can't stand sweeping, you can take care of the toilets while your friend sweeps. You might even end up enjoying yourself! Put on some music you both enjoy or a stand-up routine in the background and give yourself permission to have some fun.

If you feel weird asking someone to help you with such a big lift, just let him or her know that deal can go both ways! Offer to help clean his or her home when he or she is ready for it. Sweeten the deal by promising to bring your soundtrack with you or agreeing to take on the tasks you like least for each other.

LEND A HAND TO A NEW PARENT

If you're a parent, you know how daunting bringing a new baby home can be—especially the first one! However, you don't need to have had a baby to see how demanding a newborn can be. If you have a friend or family member who is a new parent, reach out and see if you can lend a hand.

New parents generally appreciate when you do things like bring them premade meals, help them out with chores, give them a hand with running errands, and—of course—bring them coffee! Don't limit yourself to these tasks though; they might simply want you to sit and watch the baby for a while so that they can get in a shower or do a couple loads of laundry, or maybe they would appreciate you knocking a chore off of their to-do list the most (like taking their car for an oil change or picking up some groceries).

The best way to know that your gesture will be appreciated is to ask! Find out what your loved ones would most appreciate and hop in your car to help them take a load off.

START A BOOK CLUB

If you're a reader, you already know the joys of losing yourself in a good book. Books can help you understand yourself better, learn new things, broaden your horizons, and give you a chance to relax. To take it from a fun solo activity to a healthy relationship-building activity, try starting a book club.

When you form your own book club, you have to put in a little more effort than simply joining an ongoing club, but you also get some great perks: You get to choose which books to read and whom to include! Figure out what books are on your to-read list and see if you have any friends or family members who are also interested in those books. Set up a time to meet and make the space inviting and welcoming for your guests (e.g., if you have the time, you can bake cookies beforehand).

Taking some time to do something you enjoy, meeting up with people you love, and opening yourself up for a lively and interesting discussion is one of the best ways to boost your relationships and defend against burnout.

SHOW APPRECIATION FOR YOUR FRIENDS

Do you appreciate your friends, especially when you've been leaning on them more than usual? No doubt you do, but take a moment to think about how often you show them your appreciation. We tend to get too caught up in our lives to think much about showing our friends appreciation, but it's a great way to improve the health of a relationship, and it just feels good to do!

Choose a friend (or multiple friends) that you are feeling most appreciative for and think about what you can do to show them you care. It will depend on your friend(s), but here are some good options:

- Write your friend a letter to tell him or her how much you appreciate them in your own words.
- Give your friend a small but meaningful gift.
- Help your friend with a chore or task that he or she is not excited about doing.
- Send your friend a playlist of songs you know he or she likes, or that you think he or she will like.
- Send a postcard or greeting card, just because.

When you show appreciation for your loved ones, you not only give them the warm fuzzies, you also remind yourself why you love them!

TEACH A LOVED ONE YOUR SKILL

Some say that knowledge is the best gift you can give someone, as it is one of the only things that can never be taken away. When you teach someone useful information or a valuable skill, it is something they can always carry with them. If it's a skill that they can use in everyday life, you have also given them another resource to call upon when needed.

Think about which skill you have that might be helpful for someone you love. Perhaps you're an excellent cook, great at budgeting, or handy with a hammer. Whatever your special skill is, take some time to think about how you learned it and how you can best teach it to someone else.

Now, think about who you would like to share your skill with. It may be a young person in your life, since young people are less likely to already have all the life skills they might need. Ask this person if they would like to learn your skill, and set up some time to teach them. You don't need a strict schedule or timeline, but you should make at least a loose plan to keep you both on track.

Sharing your skill will help you feel good, give you a chance to focus on something other than work or whatever it is that is stressing you out, and aid you in building a stronger bond with someone you love.

GIVE A BEAR HUG

Hugs are a quick and easy way to get a mood boost. This is because our brains release a chemical called oxytocin in response to human touch. Oxytocin, also known as the "love hormone" or "cuddle hormone," is responsible for our feelings of closeness when we're with someone we love. It helps us bond and build stronger relationships, and it also feels good when our brains give us a dose of it!

Take advantage of oxytocin's positive effects by enlisting a loved one to give you a bear hug. Regular hugs are great, but bear hugs are even more effective in enhancing our mood and making us feel loved and cared for.

Here's how to do a proper bear hug: stand facing your hug partner, wrap your arms all the way around him or her, and have him or her do the same. You can throw in some squeezes or back rubbing to enhance the hug (a kiss is also a nice addition if your hug partner is your significant other), but make sure to hold on tight for at least 15 seconds and enjoy the rush!

GO OUT FOR A FANCY MEAL WITH A FRIEND

We generally only go out to fancy or extravagant meals when we are trying to impress a date or celebrating something, but you don't have to wait for a special occasion to get dressed up and enjoy a nice meal! Taking some time to treat yourselves for no particular reason can have a big impact on your mood and your relationship, since it will feel like something special is happening.

Ask a friend to join you for a nice dinner, and reiterate there is no big reason—you just want to do something special with your friend! You can even call it a date; after all, there's no reason you can't have special dates with your friends. Just make sure to be clear about your intentions when using the word "date."

See if your friend has any burning desire to try a fancy restaurant or pick one out yourself and get his or her approval. Treat it like you would a romantic date or a big celebration: Make a reservation, dress your best, and order that expensive bottle of wine! You'll find that treating yourself and your friend to a nice date will put you in a great mood and give you a fun evening to reminisce about together, something that can come in handy when you're trying to cope with stress.

ASK A FRIEND TO HELP YOU GET HEALTHY

It's tough to get healthy on your own. If you've ever tried to lose a significant amount of weight, you know just how hard it can be! It can be especially hard when you're feeling burned out, but this is also the best time to get healthy. Getting physically healthy and spending time with a loved one makes this activity doubly effective!

To make it a little easier (and more fun), ask a friend to help you on your journey. Pick someone who is experienced with following a healthy diet and exercising, but make sure your chosen friend is also someone who can effectively motivate and encourage you. The last thing you need is someone who will make working out a chore or unintentionally make you feel bad about yourself.

Tell your friend about your goal, and ask if he or she would be interested in helping you. Work with him or her to come up with a plan that will help you succeed. Make sure to show your appreciation for your friend's help!

SURPRISE A LOVED ONE WITH A SMALL GIFT

To show your love and give your relationship a boost, consider picking out a small but meaningful gift for a friend, family member, or your significant other.

To give your gift extra impact, give the gift to your loved one on a regular day—not for a birthday, anniversary, or other celebration. It's the gifts that are unexpected that are the most memorable and often the most appreciated. Think about how you would feel if you got a meaningful gift "just because"! It would likely make you feel loved, cared for, and happy with your relationship with the giver.

Give your loved one this same feeling by picking out something you think he or she will love. You don't need to spend a ton of money on a gift to show him or her you care. What's most important is the intention behind the gift and making sure it's a meaningful one. Think about who your loved one is and what he or she enjoys, and get creative!

This will not only make your loved one feel good, it will also make you feel good and add on to your relationship, something you will be able to lean on in difficult times.

SUPPORT YOUR LOVED ONE'S GOALS

You know how you feel when someone you love offers you support and reassurance in your quest to meet your goals? You probably feel loved, encouraged, and even more motivated to work toward them. It's nice to know your efforts are acknowledged! To give your relationship with your loved one a boost, try doing the same for them.

If you don't already know what your loved one's goals are, talk to them and find out. These sorts of questions can lead to great conversations, allowing you to get to know your loved one even better. Once you figure out what their goals are, think of at least one or two ways you can show them support. For example, if their goal is to learn Spanish, get them a workbook or a gift card for their app store so they can buy a helpful app. If their goal is to lose weight, join them for a healthy homemade dinner.

Supporting your loved one in meeting their goals will make them feel loved, improve your relationship, and give you some much-needed warm and fuzzy feelings, all of which can help you defend against the symptoms of burnout.

ASK A FRIEND TO HELP YOU MOVE

Moving—we all do it eventually, and we all hate the work that comes with it! Even if you're excited to get into your new place, nobody is excited about the organizing, packing, and cleaning you have to do beforehand or the physical moving of the boxes to get your stuff to your new place.

To make your move a little bit easier, enlist a friend (or two) to help you with the moving process. If you feel bad asking someone to put in all that work, consider asking one friend to help with organizing and packing, another to help with cleaning, and another to help with the actual move. You can also offer your own assistance whenever they move to make things feel a little fairer.

Enjoy the extra set of hands and show your appreciation with some pizza and beer or another treat of their choice. To really recover from burnout and take steps to prevent it, you need to get comfortable with asking for help—and accepting it. Use this exercise to work on building that comfort.

ENLIST YOUR FRIENDS FOR A JOINT YARD SALE

Yard sales: They're no one's favorite activity (although they are generally better than moving), but they are sometimes a necessity, and they can leave you with that great feeling of being unburdened and more organized.

If you have a bunch of extra stuff just lying around and collecting dust, see if any of your loved ones are in the same boat. If they are also looking to unload some of their extra stuff, host a joint yard sale. It not only makes sense to bring everything together in one place for prospective buyers, it also lessens the burden on each of the sellers.

It might be a pain to plan and execute, but at least you'll be getting something important done and spending some time with your friends. Doing regular, everyday stuff like hosting yard sales, organizing, and cleaning can take your relationship with your friend to a new, deeper level, putting you more at ease with one another and building your sense that you can rely on one another. These are the kinds of relationships that you need most to help you dig out of the pit of burnout.

SHOW A RELATIVE HOW TO SEE THE GLASS HALF FULL

Cultivating a sense of optimism is one of the best ways to cope with the symptoms of burnout and one of the best ways to prevent future burnout. It can be tough to be optimistic on your own, but sharing your goal with a buddy can help you to stay on track.

You probably have a relative who isn't likely to see the positive in things—perhaps a cynical grandmother or a moody uncle who finds it much easier to complain than to see the good. Set your sights on this relative and set a goal to help him or her be more optimistic. Be an example for this pessimistic relative by being positive yourself and verbalizing your "glass-half-full" view.

When your relative starts going down the path of negativity, stop this person in his or her tracks and gently guide him or her toward the more positive outlook. This exercise has the added benefit of encouraging you to be more optimistic too, on top of giving you an opportunity to brighten your relative's day and inspiring him or her to be a little more upbeat.

WRITE A POEM FOR SOMEONE YOU LOVE

If you're not a poet by nature, don't worry! You don't need to be a wordsmith to write something sweet and meaningful. Look up the different types of poetry and choose a type that seems best suited to your skills.

For instance, you could write a limerick, in which the first two lines rhyme, the second two lines rhyme, and the fifth line calls back to the first two lines with its rhyme. You could also go the short and sweet route with a haiku. These are short poems, often used to express a feeling or a simple sight (like a sunset or a lake), with a specific syllable structure: the first line is five syllables, the second line is seven syllables, and the third line is five syllables.

Whichever form you choose to express your love in, make sure to put some thought into it and take it at least somewhat seriously—but not too seriously! The sweet spot is when you effectively convey your feelings but are willing to laugh at yourself at the same time. Getting to this point with someone, where you are comfortable telling them how you feel and also ready to laugh together, is an excellent resource to draw from in your fight against stress and burnout.

GIVE A TOAST TO SOMEONE IMPORTANT TO YOU

You don't need to be a master public speaker or speechwriter to give a good toast. A good toast is one that comes from the heart, gets your point across, and isn't too long! A good toast will also help you feel closer to the recipient and build trust and respect, both of which you need for a positive and meaningful relationship.

If there is a big event or celebration coming up soon, offer to make a toast. A wedding is a good place to do it, and you would also not be out of place giving a toast at a graduation, award ceremony, or the celebration for a promotion. However, if none of these events are coming up soon for the person you'd like to toast, simply stand up and give one at dinner! There's no law against it, after all.

When you write your toast, think about the things you most like and admire about this person and try to distill them down into one or two anecdotes, then connect the anecdotes back to the person's general nature. For example, you might tell a story about how he saw a car accident and stopped to check on everyone involved, then reiterate that he's a considerate and caring person.

A heartfelt toast will not only help you grow closer, it will also remind you of the most important things in life—kindness, generosity, loving relationships, and so on—all of which are essential for helping you defend yourself against burnout.

WRITE A LOVE NOTE AND HIDE IT

This is a great exercise to show your significant other your love, brighten his or her day, and build another happy memory into your relationship, which can prevent as well as improve the symptoms of burnout. Grab a piece of paper and a pen, sit down, and take a few minutes to think about your love for your partner.

Write down how you feel about your partner, and be as specific as possible. Tell your partner some of the things you love most about him or her, like his or her conversation skills, wicked sense of humor, or how attentive he or she is to you and your needs. List a few things you like about your loved one's body as well, like his or her beautiful smile or cute butt.

Once you've finished your love note, hide it somewhere where your significant other is sure to find it—and sooner rather than later. Some good ideas are in a jacket pocket, in a purse or bag, or in the nightstand. Leaving love notes for your partner is a good way to strengthen your bond and create some of those lovely warm, fuzzy feelings between you and your partner, which can go a long way toward building yourself a burnout buffer. Moments like these help you get some perspective and realize what's really important in life: love.

CHECK UP ON AN INTROVERT

The world is made up of all kinds of people that are not easily categorized, but the introvert-extrovert spectrum is a useful way to classify people that can help you better understand and work with them. You are likely friends with many people on both sides of the spectrum, but you have probably learned to treat them slightly differently based on where they fall.

For this exercise, you'll be checking up on someone closer to the introvert end of the scale. Introverts are generally a bit quieter and more reserved than extroverts, although this is not always the case; the main characteristic of introverts is that they need to be alone to recharge their batteries. After a fun night out, they might need to take the next day to relax at home.

However, for some introverts it can be easy to get too comfortable at home and feel "stuck." To make sure this doesn't happen to one of your introvert friends, text him or her or call to see if you can drop by and check in. It could be exactly what he or she needed in that moment!

It can also give you a better understanding of introversion and the need to take some time for yourself. Both extroverts and introverts need healthy relationships to help them recover from and defend against burnout.

GET INTROSPECTIVE WITH AN EXTROVERT

Unlike your introvert friend, your extrovert friends likely don't need you to check in to make sure they aren't hibernating. To enhance your relationship with an extrovert, try to get him or her thinking outside of his or her box.

Extroverts generally make sure they get enough face-to-face time with other people, but they may lack in introspection what they have in spades when it comes to external interaction. Although it's just a general rule and there are many exceptions, many extroverts can use a little prompting to reflect and think about their inner workings.

To help extroverts get introspective, have a discussion with them that encourages them to dive deep and think about *what* they think and *how* they think. Ask them questions about themselves and ask about the lessons they have learned. Conversations like these will help you to better understand your friends and give you all practice in listening and understanding different perspectives, traits that make you a better friend, partner, and family member.

GO ON A SPIRITUAL RETREAT WITH A LOVED ONE

Spiritual retreats aren't for everyone, but if you are one of those people who find meaning and purpose in spirituality, it might be right up your alley! These retreats offer you a chance to sit quietly, think about the important things in life, and explore your spirituality.

To get even more out of the experience, consider inviting a loved one to attend a retreat with you. It's best if this person is at least somewhat interested in spirituality, but all he or she really needs to get something out of the experience is an open-mind.

At the retreat, attend the events together, ask questions, and discuss your thoughts about what you're learning. Sit and listen together. Sit in silence together. Sit in prayer or meditation together. Laugh together, cry together, and grow together.

Attending a spiritual retreat with someone you love will open your mind, enhance your bond, and leave you with lots of thoughts about what is most valuable to you in life. In turn, keeping your focus on what is important to you will protect you from the stress and worry that lead to burnout.

DO SOMETHING YOUR FRIEND ENJOYS

We all like to do things we enjoy with our friends, but it's important to set aside some time to do things our friends enjoy too. The best relationships are built on mutual interests and a willingness to compromise—relationships in which both participants are eager to make the other happy, however they can.

To build (or deepen) a relationship like this, make sure to spend some quality time with your friend doing what he or she wants to do. If you're not sure what your friends want, ask them! Some people are overly agreeable, making it hard to tell what they really prefer. If your friend is one of these easygoing people, engage him or her in discussion to find out what he or she likes, then make it a point to do it!

Doing something you wouldn't normally do is a great way to show your friend you care. As an added bonus, it's a great way to figure out new things you like and be a little more open-minded. Invest in your relationships by doing things for and with your friends, and you will end up with a rock-solid resource, someone that you can rely on when you're going through tough times or teetering on the edge of burnout.

DO SOMETHING YOU ENJOY (WITH FRIENDS)

It's a wonderful idea to do things you normally wouldn't have any interest in doing for the sake of your loved ones. For example, attending a lecture or service about a topic you don't really care about shows your loved one his or her interests are important to you, and seeing a movie you aren't interested in but your friend is dying to see is a sweet gesture.

However, it's important that you don't go too far in one direction; you should never have a relationship where you always do what the other person wants to do. Even if you're easygoing and willing to follow your friend's lead, there should be at least some occasions when you both do something you enjoy.

Doing things you enjoy is not only fun for you, it also gives you a chance to shine, since you are always more enthusiastic and eager about things you like to do. Further, it helps you create more positive memories with your friends, which solidifies your friendships and gives you a good foundation on which to build an ever deeper and more meaningful relationship. Don't always "go with the flow," make sure your friends care about your happiness too! This is how you ensure that you surround yourself with strong social support—a surefire way to build your defenses against burnout.

PLAN AND COOK A MEAL TOGETHER

This is a task that many couples do already, but it can be hard to find the time or the energy when you're feeling burned out. It takes a bit of prep, but the payoff is worth it.

Ask your significant other to set aside some time to plan, prepare, and eat a nice meal together. Make sure you head to the grocery store or farmers' market and pick up all the supplies you need, so neither of you need to run out at the last minute.

Decide which of you is going to do which job, or let things naturally work themselves out, whichever style best suits you! The important thing is to work together to prepare and cook the food so that you both feel invested in the meal and a sense of pride in the results.

Once you have it ready, open a nice bottle of wine or pour yourself some other special drink and sit down to enjoy it. Don't allow any talk of work, side projects, kids, family responsibilities, or any other boring everyday topics. Instead, treat it like the special evening it is and use the time to reconnect and rekindle your bond.

COUNT THE SMALL STUFF

When you get down to it, the small stuff is the stuff that really matters. You shouldn't sweat the small stuff, but you also shouldn't ignore it; the small stuff is what builds up to create a great day, a great week, and a great life.

Enlist a loved one to help you count the small stuff. Agree to take note of all the good small things you come across in your day. If it helps, you can write it down in a journal or diary app so you don't forget. Pay attention to things like the mild weather, the person who let you in when you were in bad traffic, and the sweet smile you got from the barista at your favorite coffee shop.

At the end of the day, you'll have a list of all the good little things that happened during your day rather than a list of complaints or annoying things that threw off your mood. Compare your list with your loved one, discuss the effects that these small good things had on you and your mood, and point out any that you may have missed.

Doing this regularly will help you have a more positive outlook, which will help you be more resilient when bouncing back from difficulty or failure. Building your resilience will ensure that you are ready to combat the cause of burnout and fend off unnecessary stress.

ASK YOUR SIGNIFICANT OTHER FOR A FOOT MASSAGE

If you don't have time for a full body or back massage, you can go with the less intensive option: a foot rub. Foot rubs are great for relieving your stress, encouraging relaxation, and showing care and love for your partner.

When you're feeling burned out, you'll need some quality time with loved ones as well as some physical self-care to recover. Asking your significant other to treat you to a foot massage is a good way to get both of these needs met.

Ask nicely (and offer to return the favor at a future date) and explain why you could use a foot rub. If your partner has the time and is understanding of your current struggles, he or she should jump at the chance to do something nice for you!

Have your partner focus on the arch of the foot especially, as this part of the body is a pressure point that is connected to many other areas; as such, rubbing it can induce blissful relaxation throughout the body. Make sure to prepare your partner with some lotion or coconut oil to really kick the experience up a notch.

HIT UP A FARMERS' MARKET

Going to the farmers' market is a great idea for a cheap date or friend outing—depending on how much you like fruits and veggies! Farmers' markets are free to browse and there are usually at least one or two conveniently located in most areas with tons of yummy produce to choose from.

Take your loved one out for a stroll on a bright, sunny morning or afternoon and take your time looking through all the wares that the sellers have to offer. You can make it into a game by guessing what the other person's favorite item will be and buying it for them to enjoy. Alternatively, one person can pick out three of his or her favorite fruits or vegetables, and the other person can use all three ingredients in a dish that afternoon or evening.

Enjoy the weather, enjoy the stroll, and enjoy spending some quality time with your loved one—just don't forget to bring your reusable shopping bags for any fresh, tasty purchases you make! This exercise helps you with two of the most important factors in preventing and healing from burnout: eating healthy and maintaining good relationships.

GIVE A GENUINE COMPLIMENT

Genuine compliments are amazing to receive, since they are prompted by the compliment giver's open and honest consideration of the receiver, and they come from a place of authentic appreciation. It feels great when you get a genuine compliment because it means someone is seeing you for who you really are, and that he or she likes you for who you really are.

To spread that love and appreciation to someone else, give one of your loved ones a genuine compliment. Think about what you love about this person and what his or her best qualities are, and pick one of them to focus on. Consider what the receiver would want to hear as well—after all, a compliment is only as good as how the receiver interprets it! Make sure your compliment is clear and with no string attached or qualifications (e.g., not a backhanded or passive-aggressive compliment).

When you give someone a compliment that is authentic and from the heart, the receiver can *tell* that it's real and from the heart. Giving a compliment like this will improve your relationship with your loved one and boost his or her self-confidence, but it can also have the added effect of getting you to look at the world with a more positive filter; when you look for positive things in others, they're much easier to spot. This more positive filter will make it much harder for stress and burnout to bring you down.

PRACTICE COMPROMISE

Compromise is perhaps the greatest art and the most important feature in a healthy relationship, but it can also take some practice to get right. To make sure you are approaching things with the right mindset, practice compromising with those you love.

It's great to find a win-win solution (one in which both parties get exactly what they want), but sometimes there is no win-win to be found. It would be great if all problems could be solved with winning solutions for everybody involved, but it's just not possible to always win! In those cases, you need to compromise in order to obtain the best possible outcome. Compromise might mean that sometimes you get what you want while the other person does not, or your partner gets what he or she wants while you do not.

Try looking at things from your partner's point of view, considering his or her wants and needs while balancing them with your own, and coming up with creative solutions for the toughest problems. You'll be happy you did, as learning how to compromise greatly improves a relationship and gives you both greater trust and respect of one another. Practicing compromise will help you build the kind of relationship you need to support yourself and protect yourself from burnout.

MAKE AND DELIVER BREAKFAST IN BED

Breakfast in bed: It isn't just for Mother's Day! You can make any day a super special one for you and your partner by making some homemade breakfast and delivering it to your sweetheart while he or she is in bed. Make sure he or she will still be in bed when you're done, and try to keep him or her from waking or rising before the food is ready. Coming into the bedroom and surprising your partner with a custom-cooked breakfast is a wonderful feeling, and one that will likely be repaid!

Find out which breakfast foods your significant other prefers and plan on cooking that. Make sure to check the recipe the night before so you don't hit any unexpected snags and you're not missing any of the basics, like eggs, flour, or olive oil.

To kick it up a notch, find out what flowers, music, or small items your significant other would enjoy and incorporate them into breakfast. You can have his or her favorite songs playing in the background or complement the meal with a small but meaningful and thoughtful gift.

Activities like these will strengthen your bond and give you a safeguard against burnout by keeping you focused on what is most important in life: your loved ones.

MAKE A DONATION IN YOUR LOVED ONE'S NAME

If you don't have a ton of time, but you want to do something nice for your friend, consider making a donation to your favorite charity (or his or her favorite charity) in his or her name. It's an easy and classy move that shows your loved one that you care. It also funds important services or charity work that you find personally meaningful—and hopefully work that your loved one finds meaningful as well.

Making a donation in someone's name can help you beat burnout in three ways:

1. It is a nice gesture for your friend, which will likely make your friend happy.

2. You will see your friend's appreciation and feel good about your gesture, which can enhance and deepen your friendship.

3. It is an altruistic act, which will likely give you those nice, warm, fuzzy feelings and boost your mood.

Feeling good about yourself, enhancing your friendship, and boosting your mood can all contribute to a healthier you, and a healthier you is much more capable of combating the symptoms of burnout! Remember that you don't have to donate a ton of money to make a difference—even a few dollars can have a big impact.

INDEX